MELODY OF BHAKTI AND ENLIGHTENMENT

Melody of Bhakti and Enlightenment

Dr. R.N. Vyas, M.A., Ph.D., D.Litt., LL. B., S.R.
Director
Academy of Social Thought, Indore

COSMO PUBLICATIONS

NEW DELHI INDIA

1983

First Published 1983

Published by

Rani Kapoor (Mrs.)
COSMO PUBLICATIONS
24-B, Ansari Road, Daryaganj
New Delhi-110002 (India)

Printed at

Shabdankan Printers,
Delhi-110053.

FOREWORD

I have gone through your book 'Melody of Bhakti and Enlightenment.' Only a Bhakt can go so deep into this subject. I congratulate you for bringing out this beautiful topic so elaborately. In Satyug, Dwapar, Treta, to achieve enlightenment of God one had to do great tapasya, but in Kaliyug our Rishis have shown this easy way for liberation of human being. You have touched all the shakhas of Bhakti Movement. I pray to God that this book will have a distinguished place in the literature. Your approach and conclusion is deep and wide in a simple manner.

With best wishes,

Yours Sincerely
B. D. Sharma

PREFACE

I feel pleasure in placing the present work in the hands of my learned readers. Bhakti is a unique contribution of India to the world. Indian culture has been given a specific dimension by Bhakti. Though highest knowledge has been preached by the Upanishads, it is a historical paradox that they did not reach the minds of average people. It is Bhakti which reached them and gave them a sublime attitude towards the world. That is why Indians are mostly tolerant and catholic in religion, politics and social outlook. Hinduism has place for everybody, from the stark materialist like a Chārvaka to a Vedāntī who dismisses the universe as a Māyā, a mere empirical reality.

I have tried to study the nature of Bhakti in the present work and have established that it is based on a firm foundation of highest knowledge. It contains a capacity of destroying ego of an individual that paves way for the onward march on the lofty path of spiritual advancement.

I am sure that whosoever wants to understand the nature of Indian culture must first understand the nature of devotion. The present work has taken a long period in its completion. It, therefore, embodies my endeavour to understand the nature of Bhakti running in many years. That is why I have a special liking for this work of mine. I hope that the readers too shall like it. I am grateful to the publishers for publishing it and for making it possible for me to present it to my readers.

Academy of Social Thought
INDORE

R. N. Vyas

Tvadīyaṁ Vastu Govinda Tubhyameva Samarpaye

GOD IS ONE, YET MANY

"He is smaller than an atom, and bigger than the Himalayas. He is contained even in a drop of the ocean, and yet not even the seven seas can encompass Him.

"Reason is powerless to know Him. He is beyond the reach or grasp of reason. Faith is essential in this matter.

"My faith runs so very much faster than my reason that I can challenge the whole world and say :
'God is, was and ever shall be.'

. . . .

"But those who want to deny His existence are at liberty to do so. He is Merciful and Compassionate. He is not an earthly king needing an army to make us accept His sway.

"He allows us freedom, and yet His compassion commands obedience to His will.

"But if any one of us disdains to bow to His will, He says: 'So be it. My sun will shine no less for thee, my clouds will rain no less for thee. I need not force thee to accept my sway.'

"Of such a God, let the ignorant dispute the existence. I am one of the millions of wise men who believe in Him, and are never tired of bowing to Him and singing His glory."

—*Mahatma Gandhi*

(*Quoted from "God Is Truth", published by Bharatiya Vidya Bhavan, Bombay, India*)

Like birdlings unfledged unto their mother,
Like hungry calves unto the cow's udder,
Like the anxious beloved unto her far off lover,
O, Lotus-eyed Lord, does my mind long to see Thee.

—*The Bhāgavata*

CONTENTS

1

Nature of Bhakti

O World, thou choosest not the better part.
It is not wisdom to be only wise,
And on the inward vision close the eyes,
But it is wisdom to believe the heart.

—Santayana

Give all to love;
Obey thy heart;
Friends, kindred, days,
Estate, good-fame,
Plans, credit, and the Muse-
Nothing refuse.

—Ralph Waldo Emerson

"If we wish to know the inner nature of Reality we must resort to the whole personality of which intellect is only a part."

—Radhakrishnan
in
An Idealist View of Life.

Devotion and Psychology

Before attempting to understand the purport and importance of devotion, we should try to understand the psychology of devotion. Human personality is a complex of three dominant tendencies which can be described as cognition (knowledge), affection (feeling) and action (will). Just as the Sāṁkhya system believes that the world is constituted by the Satva, Rajas and Tamas elements, in the same manner, psychologically even human personality is a bundle of the abovementioned three elements. Of course, these elements are not present in the same degree of proportion. In some persons, the element of knowledge is dominant and therefore he becomes a rationalist, in some other persons affection is dominant and therefore they are persons of emotions and feeling, while in the rest the element of willing is dominant and therefore they are men of action.

In the domain of spiritual pursuits, too, we have three types of persons. Those in whom knowledge dominates, they become philosophers and assert that the Supreme cannot be realized without reason or knowledge (ṛte jñānāt na muktiḥ). Others in whom the current of feeling is dominant believe that the Supreme can be realized only through devotion or a sense of deep-attachment to the God. And the rest believe that the Supreme can be realized only through rituals and prescribed acts like the fasting, prayer, visiting the holy places, serving the purohitas and priests. But these categories are not mutually exclusive and therefore persons belonging to a category can move to another category depending on their social, family and mental environments. But usually persons stick to their mental habits and an element of rationalization helps them in confining them to their own self-accepted category.

The substance of this analysis is that persons belonging to different categories have a tendency of asserting that their approach alone is the best. Though it is not possible to satisfy everybody belonging to the divergent groups, yet it is possible to weigh the positive and negative points found in each of the above mentioned stands.

Upholders of knowledge are right in some respects. Man has been endowed with a brain by nature. It is not irrational to seek guidance from our reason. Lack of rational attitude leads a man to blind faith and inhuman acts like offering a human being as sacrifice to some god or goddess. Lack of reason has created walls of hatred in human society even in the region of religion. Bloody battles have been fought and tax on the acceptance of a different faith has been imposed. Innocent people have been butchered. Every sensible man is aware of the pages of history that have been dyed in human blood in the name of religion.

But though we accept the importance of reason in the domain of religion under the circumstances, we must not forget that thoughts lack the strength of faith. Even if, for example, we reason out the nature of Supreme Reality as an abstract Absolute, we lack the strength of a feeling in following that difficult path. People have merety decried the attempts to prove the existence of God through reason, but they have lacked the warmth of human friendliness, a strength to sacrifice the whole world like Mīrā for the sake of one's Lord. Even if for arguments' sake, we concede that it is possible to establish the existence of God through reason and argument, we shall get nothing, for the warmth of feeling cannot be found in cold logic. Like Duryodhana, the notorious Kaurava, man shall say that though the path of divinity is known to him, he cannot follow it; and though the path of irreligion too is known to him, he cannot resist following that path. Hence mere reasoning would not lead us to our destined destination of liberation. The path of feeling has the advantage of giving solid strength to follow the path of devotion despite every odd or difficulty. However, the lack of knowledge may lead a person to follow an irrational path. It can lead to a vain sacrifice and destruction of human society. And the path of rituals lacks the solid foundation of the path of knowledge, and keeps a person on the lowest rung of spiritual development. Rituals may be of help to a beginner, but if they are not transcended, they block the way of spiritual development. Just as the clothes of a child cannot be of any use to him when he grows up or learning of alphabets through concrete objects like "A for apple" cannot serve the purpose of a grown up person, in the same manner, the path of rituals cannot be followed by the mature. If we want to have a dependable means of spiritual development, we must combine the best elements found in the three paths outlined above. The good aspects of all must be synthesised. And that can be done only in the path of devotion. In the words of Rāmānuja, devotion is 'bhaktirupāpanna jñānam' i.e. the knowledge that has matured in the form of devotion. Vallabha states that devotion is a firm and all-surpassing affection for God with a sense of His Greatness. Sankara is of the opinion that devotion implies attainment of soul's real nature. Thus an element of higher knowledge is invariably present in devotion. It also accommodates idol worship, temple worship etc. as a means of developing devotion. Thus devotion signifies a synthesis of the best elements of knowledge, feeling and willing. Gross devotion is no real devotion. Real devotion implies the growth of whole personality of a person in the right direction. Moreover, it is easy to follow it, as 99% people are slaves of their emotions and feeling. A Rasakhana who loved a Baniya youth, Sūrdāsa who loved a prostitute, Tusalīdāsa who loved his own wife, all found it easy to direct their affection to the feet of their Lord.

Qualities of a Devotee

Devotion has been understood as supreme attachment for the Lord. It involves a sense of detachment from the worldly objects. A devotee has many qualities which are not found in a person attached to mundane objects. He has humility, boastlessness, egolessness, harmlessness, fearlessness truthfulness, angerlessness, a sense of friendship towards all, tenderness for all, compassion for all, absence of enmity for anybody, greedlessness, dispassion, forgiveness for the wrongs done by others, straightforwardness, non-greediness, steadiness, spiritedness, sex-restraint, non-stealing, non-hoarding, purity of body and mind, renunciation, charitableness, endurance, desirelessness, contentment, equipoise of mind, taciturnity, undisturbability by joy or grief, unaffected attitude by praise or hatred, love for enmity, buoyancy, equality towards all, indifference to the three guṇas viz. satva, rajas and tamas, tranquility, awareness of the defects of worldly life and events like birth, death, old age and disease, lack of attachment for his near and dear like wife, progeny house etc., universal benevolence, study of holy books and scriptures, purity of mind etc. Such innumerable qualities of a devetee have been mentioned in the Bhagavadgītā (chapters ii, iii, iv, vi, xii, xiii, xiv, xvii) The Bhāgavata states that a devotee is kindhearted, free from any sense of animosity towards anybody, forebearing and patient, truthful to the core of his heart, equal to all, impartial, benefactor of all, self-restrained, lovable, affable, morally perfect, selfless. He does not eat much and loves peace. He does not make mistakes and is sober in mind. He never loses fortitude and courage. He is the controller of six guṇas viz. hunger, thirst, sorrow, attachment, birth and death. He never seeks any honour for himself, but always tries to give respect to others. He is very expert in making others understand the truth about God and is friendly to all. He is full of sympathy and pity for others. He does not care for the Vedic injunctions and rites and rituals and is a servant of God, leaving all other religious conventions. (Bhāgavata 11-11-29 to 33). We can say that he leads a life that is completely detached from the worldly life and is free from every tinge of selfishness, and is perfectly attached to the Lord. (Bhāgavata 8-1-10)

A devotee is an abode of many peerless qualities. He has independence, efficiency, patience, boldness altruism, gravity, heroism, strength, hospitability, restraint of senses . Endurance implies a capacity to bear pain, contentment implies the conquest of greed, charity means the non-punishment of the offender, heroism means the conquest of lower tendencies of mind, truthfulness for him is equality towards all and agreeable speech in conformity with truth. He considers it foolishness to identify the self with the body and its organs. His happiness consists in transcending the realms of pleasure and pain. For him suffering means dependence on desire and pleasure. For him real wealth consists of possession of good qualities. Poverty does not mean absence or want of money. It means discontentment. For him slavery implies an attachment to the mean tendencies of mind. The ideal of a devotee is to be attached to the Lord, who is our only Friend and Master. And what is wisdom ? Wisdom does not mean accumulating material wealth or seeking worldly gains. Wisdom is the true knowledge of bondage and salvation. (Bhāgavata 11-19-33 to 44).

The Nārada Bhakti Sūtra has summarised the qualities of a devotee by stating that he should not listen to talks about women, wealth and the conduct of atheists (Sūtra 63.) He should give up egotism, pride etc. (Sūtra 64). He should consecrete all conduct to the Lord and make him the object of his lust, resentment, pride etc. (Sūtra 64). Argumentation about the Truth and devotion to the Lord should not be undertaken by him (Sūtra 74). Bhakti Sastra, i.e. teachings on devotion, should be studied intelligently and path of devotion should be studied intelligently, and observances enjoined therein should be perforned (Sūtra 76). We should not waste our time in the enjoyment of earthly pleasures, gains etc. and should devote our entire attention and energy in the pursuit of devotion (S. 77). Harmlessness, truthfulness purity, kindness, faith and other excellent qualities of character a devotee has to develop (S. 78). If the Lord is invoked with a single minded attention and devotion, He at once reveals Himself and fills the heart of the devotee with divine presence (S. 79, 80).

If we try to analyse the qualities of a devotee we find that he is a selfless man. His wealth, energy, strength, powers, intelligence etc. are devoted to the Lord and hence to every being of the universe. He loves every being, because he finds his Lord in every being. The sorrow of others is his sorrow, and the happiness of others is his happiness. His wants are very limited and he is ready to sacrifice everything for the poor in whom he sees his Lord, the Daridra Nārāyana.

Such a devotee is the biggest benefactor of society, because his heart is free from greed, lust, hatred, spirit of exploitation selfisness, laziness etc. His strength protects society from the fierce dangers, and his activeness brings warmth to society. If for a moment, we doubt the very existence of God and suppose Him to be a matter of individual fiction, illusion or hallucination, still because of the excellent and rare qualities found in devotees, we shall have to concede that God must exist. And if He does not exist, he should exist. Faith in the Lord and devotion to Him are so rewarding for the individual and the society that a faith in God's existence appears to be desirable and necessary.

Our modern culture has banished God and in the process has brought in a stultifying environment where crookedness prevails and exploitation rules to such an extent that even our communism, socialism and democracy become words without meaning and ideologies without content.

Concept of Bhakti

Though I am not inexperienced in the domain of writing I must confess that to give exact connotation of Bhakti is not easy. It is something that can be understood only through an inner experience. However, some attempt has to be made to make the concept of Bhakti as intellible as possible.

In this context a mention of human psychology is necessary. That will help us in understanding the meaning of devotion (Bhakti) to some extent.

Psychologically speaking, human mind is constituted by the elements of cognition, affection and conation. No mental construct and act; therefore, is free from the combination of these entities. But while we admit that every mental act of a human being bears an impact of these three factors, we cannot state that every act contains the same proportion of these elements. In one mental act, cognition or thinking is predominant, while in the other affection or feeling may be dominant. It is just like Saṁkhya theory which asserts that everything of this universe is a combination of the satva, rajas and tamas elements, but everything has differing combination of these elements.

In the realm of our spiritual or philosophical pursuits, too, this principle holds good. We should not forget this important fact. We have many paths of God realization. But if we care to pay an attention to the principal ones, there are merely three.

The three traditional paths of God realization which have been called the path of jñāna or knowledge, the path of bhakti or devotion, and the path of karma and action, correspond to the basic constituents of human mind *viz.* cognition, affection and conation respectively. But since no mental act is free from the combination of the three elements mentioned above, the three paths of God realization, too, must be replete with the combination of the three ingredients. Thus psychologically, the path of jñāna or knowledge is not totally free from the traces of devotion (bhakti) and action (karma), and the path of devotion is not totally free from the traces of knowledge and action. Our action is obviously the result of the combination of knowledge and devotion. The distinguishing marks of the three paths are the difference and distinction of the emphasis put on knowledge, devotion or action.

It is very important to remember this fact. In the absence of a clear recognition of this fact, we are likely to think that knowledge, devotion, and action are exclusive, and some may go to the extent of declaring them as contradictory to even. This, as is clear, would be a very untenable position.[1]

Out of the three paths of God realization, which should be considered the best path ? It is clear that an answer to this question would depend on the attitude of the person answering the question. But objectively speaking, we can place the path of action at the lowest level. It is not meant that the path of action is undesirable. What is meant is that since the path of action implies merely following the scriptural injunctions faithfully,[2] it is merely the stage from which a person may begin his social and spiritual life. If a person ceases to advance, that is, if his progress is retarded he is likely to become a tradition-seeker alone. At the higher stage one shall have to prefer the path of either devotion or knowledge or both. While the path of knowledge is undoubtedly very tough and difficult to follow[3], because it demands an eradication of those impulses which bind us to the world, the path of devotion is easy to follow.[4] Devotion implies sublimation of natural tendencies. We need not eradicate the instinct of sex, anger, fear or anything else of the type. Devotion demands just directing these natural urges and currents to the supreme and the miracle would take place. The gross shall turn into the fine, and the mundane into the spiritual. Our mind shall attain a rare and sublime spiritual height and we shall be drawn closest to our Beloved, our Master.[5] Thus we find that while the path of action keeps us at the lowest level, the path of knowledge, too, cannot be very helpful to an average man. The path of knowledge demands of sacrifice of the carnal and not a sanctification of the mundane. It is not only difficult for a lay man to achieve, and disheartens his determination to move on the mountainous tracts of knowledge; but goes still further and presents a terrible psychological threat to the psychological personality of a person. A superficial eradication of impulses and natural urges may degrade individuals spiriually and throw their minds in the cockpit of mental aberrations and abnormalities. Temperamentally, therefore, an average man likes to shun the path of knowledge and aspires for a route that can suit his psychological set-up ideally.

Sometimes it is thought that the path of knowledge is superior to the path of devotion. I think that there is no justifiable ground for such an attitude. Let us be fair and "not make a fetish of reason as the rationalists in their sense of dignity for man as a rational being have done."[6] If to realize the Supreme is the sole objective of human life, any medium through which he can be realized easily and conveniently is proper and desirable. In devotion we find this very easiness and natural feasibility. How can we decry devotion, then, from the point of view of an enlightened reflection ?

Moreover, human feelings are more potent than the element of intellectuality. They can transform the entire human personality, once they are aroused. Human intellectuality, on the other hand, finds itself, at times, quite feeble. We all know the famous statement of Duryodhana, the principal villain of the Mahābhārata : "I know what is truth, but I cannot follow it; I know what is untruth, but I cannot forsake it."[7] Most of us share this frailty with Duryodhana whether we accept it or not.

Jñāna, knowledge, is like the classical music of India which we admire and yet cannot appreciate heartily. It requires a very intensive practice to cultivate the tendency of appreciating it. Bhakti, devotion, on the other hand, is like the light music which moves the heart of an average man. To assert that only the classical music is the true music and the light music is no music at all, is as illogical as it is absurd. The element of music is as much present in the light music as is present in the classical type of music. Who can deny that the basic quality of music is a capacity of moving human heart and generating an enthralling experience in mind ?

Bhakti, devotion, can also be understood by taking another illustration. It is like vapour, while jñāna, knowledge, is like water. Just as vapour is produced from water and yet is different from the latter because of its great strength that can move the biggest engine and produce electricity, in the same way bhakti is produced from some kind of knowledge due to the heat generated by the affection for the sun of the Supreme and generates the electricity of lovable sentiments that kindles the light in the darkness of human hearts.

So powerful is the upsurge of human affection for the Supreme that even the highest person of the domain of knowledge feels its impact. Bacon expressed this very fact when he declared : "A little philosophy inclineth man's mind to atheism, but depth in philosophy bringeth men's minds about to religion."[8] And once its impact is felt, we find that the differences that characterise the intellectual expositions of the path of truth are melted into a throbbing unity of feeling and affection. The differences and divergences are transmuted into a warm-hearted unity. And then even Śaṁkara, a paragon of the man of knowledge, exclaims "Though the Lord of Yadus appears embodied and situated at one place, yet (in fact) He is Truth, Knowledge, and Bliss, pervading the universe, and the soul of all.[9]

Śaṁkara forgets that his philosophy, an intellectual construct, shall not allow him to deviate from his path of astute knowledge. But who can control the heart's dictates ? And when Śaṁkara exclaims like this he comes so close to Rāmānuja who states :

"I bow unto Viṣṇu, who has as His body all the sentient and non-sentient beings, who is the Self of all objects, who is associated with Śrī and who is the ocean of bliss untainted with impurity."[10]

And Vallabha comes closer to both Śaṁkara and Rāmānuja when he writes :

"I seek the shelter of Kṛṣṇa, Hari, who is perfect bliss"[11] and

"There is no God other than Kṛṣṇa, free from blemishes."[12]

This fact reveals the basic feature of devotion, which sometimes goes unnoticed. It indicates that in the temple of devotion differences are sunk completely and a unity of feeling and an integration of hearts are brought into being. I have already drawn the attention of the learned readers to this remarkable feature of devotion. Let us concede that this in itself is no insignificant achievement for devotion. The ideal of knowledge is a life that is untainted with any trace of worldly attachment because without a sense of discrimination one cannot attain the ultimate objective of knowledge viz. the detachment from the mundane objects which are just the creation of avidyā,[13] transcending the frontiers of the material world. The ideal aimed at by the follower of the path of knowledge is the realization of the nonduality of the Brahman realizing that everything other than the Brahman is just false or illusion.[14]

This objective of a nonattached life can be inculcated through the pathway of devotion more easily and naturally. A devotee who has dedicated everything to the Lord, whose self-surrender is complete and each of whose activities is just a propitiation of the Lord[15] lives a life that is dedicated in every sense of the term and is perfectly nonattached in nature.[16]

Even the identity with the Supreme, whom a man of knowledge prefers to address as the Brahman, is attained through the pathway of devotion when a devotee rises to the highest flight just as the Gopīs did in their heartiest affection for their Lord and became Kṛṣṇa themselves.[17]

But let us add here that though the path of devotion is no simple because it demands nothing else but a sense of trust and dedication to the Supreme[18], and is so pleasant as it is directed towards the Giver of bliss[19], yet it is so difficult for a person who is incapable of such a spirit of dedication. Even the great men of meditation[20] find it difficult to attain it. Yes, it is so difficult for those who cannot repose full confidence in the Supreme and His bountiful nature. A person who has been fed on the ideas that the Supreme is beyond the reach of human thought and speech even, and who is Truth, Knowledge, and Bliss alone,[21] cannot imagine even, say nothing about believing it, that the Supreme can be attained through a spirit of dedication. But the shortcut to the realization of the Brahman is known to a person of devotion because of his faith, unflinching and unwavering faith.[22]

If we can kindle this fire of faith, our ultimate objective of attaining the Lord shall be conveniently realized. Devotion, thus, draws us nearer to the Supreme, the Ultimate Truth in its peculiar and characteristic manner.

We can safely conclude that devotion is capable of realizing the objective set forth by meditation and knowledge and hence it can help a man in rising to the highest stage of spirituality.

There is still another positive trait of devotion which may be mentioned here. The world in which we have been bodily born, the society which has helped us in strengthening our body, protecting it from many outside perils and diseases and has paved the way of our spiritual progress by offering sterling aid in the inculcation of knowledge and brightening up of our mental heritage, cannot be disregarded totally even by a follower of the path of knowledge. Even Śaṁkara proclaimed the Vyāvahārika sattā or empirical existence of the world to distinguish it from an illusion. It is unfortunate, from the point of view of the world, that a man of knowledge exhibits a tendency of renouncing the world when he rises higher and higher in the domain of knowledge. He sacrifices the "world" to attain the final truth of his conception. He is perfectly justified in his approach from the point of view of his own standpoint and the ultimate Truth of his own description. But the world, too, has every right to complain that a person who is its product, who has been brought up with care and affection, and, let us add, hope, by the world and the human society, has not done justice by sticking to his own salvation and dismissing the whole world as a creation of ignorance. For an average man, therefore, the way of renunciation is not a relishable attitude. It would certainly soothe the wounded heart of humanity to see that a person who has risen to the highest rung of the ladder of spirituality should stay down, come down, to help the uninitiated and the ignorant in finding out the path of not only salvation but also of social solidarity and health.

At the present moment of history when humanity is bewildered at the invention of the most dreadful and deadly weapons of war, when the politician is using the scientist to contaminate the earth, the water and the air, when the riches of the world are being wasted in a most wanton manner in the production of the Atom Bomb and the H-bomb, when the process of an emasculation of human culture and personality is being carried out in a most outrageous fashion, when the man is being misled into the wilderness of disasters and catastrophes, and when the worth of human life has been reduced to the life of a mosquito, the world must feel the necessity of such an enlightened help all the more.

Here the man of metaphysical knowledge would, perhaps, refuse to oblige the world. But the man of sincere devotion shall be certainly prepared to sacrifice everything, including his liberation, for the welfare of humanity. Let us not forget that Prahlāda, the paragon of the devotees, clearly stated to his Lord: "I do not like to be liberated leaving the bulk of humanity behind plunged in the ocean of grief and sorrow."[23] Gandhiji refused to go to the Himalayas to seek his God. He preferred to serve Him through the service of unhappy humanity.

The man of devotion cries :

"Leave this chanting and singing and telling of beads. Whom dost thou worship in this lonely dark corner of a temple with doors all shut ?

Open thine eyes and see thy God is not before thee.
He is there where the tiller is tilling the hard ground and where the path-maker is breaking stones.
He is with them in sun and in shower, and his garment is covered with dust.
Put off thy holy mantle and even like him come down on the dusty soil.
Deliverance ? Where is this deliverance to be found?
Our master himself has joyfully taken upon him the bonds of creation; he is bound with us all for ever.
Come out of thy meditation and leave aside thy flowers and incense.
What harm is there if thy clothes become tattered and stained?
Meet him and stand by him in toil and in sweat of thy brow ?"[24]

For a devotee there is no religion higher than service of others, the whole human community.[25]

A devotee is, therefore, bound to usher the spring of prosperity and health in human society where justice shall prevail, mutual help shall be the law, and sincerity in action and conduct shall be the rule, where the exploitation of every description shall end, and humanity shall be able to smile with bright pleasure and hearty gladness.

It is an outstanding feature of Indian outlook that it has always given due importance to life and has never underestimated its worth. "The human body which is the primal source of all attainments is a well-built boat, so hard to secure and so cheap when once attained."[26]

Therefore the standpoint adopted by a man of devotion is justifiable from every point of view.

By the way, it may be mentioned that devotion serves still another purpose. It makes individual life happy and radiant. A man of devotion who reposes absolute trust in the strength and helpful nature of the Lord, is untouched by perturbation and leads a very sensible and psychologically sane life in this world of frustrations and worries, failures and defeats, poverty and exploitation. In this context it would be desirable to quote the opinion of Gandhiji :

> A man of prayer must know no disappointment because he knows that the times are in His hands who is the Arch Planner and does everything in His good time. A man of prayer, therefore, waits in faith and patience always.
>
> Making the theme of his after-prayer discourse the song that had been sung at the prayer, Gandhiji explained how the song gave the allegorical story of the struggle between the elephant king (Gajendra) and the Graha (the alligator). It was taken from the classical episode of Gajendra Moksha from the Bhagavata. The original was a piece of rare poetical merit, combining as it did the melodious music of verse with loftiness of the sentiment which it embodied. That was the test of all great pieces of art. It must combine beauty with use. Cattle might be satisfied with filling their bellies with fodder. But man liked his food to please the eye as well as provide nourishment.
>
> In the allegory of Gajendra and Graha, Gandhiji went on to explain, the elephant king was seized unawares by the crocodile as he went to have a drink of water in the river and was dragged down. The more he struggled, the deeper he sank. A stage was, however, reached when despairing of his physical prowess, he threw himself on God's grace entirely and invoked His aid, and the Lord of Dwaraka came in the twinkling of an eye and rescued him. The moral of the story, said Gandhiji, is that God never fails His devotees in the hour of trial. The condition is that there must be a living faith and the uttermost reliance on Him. The test of faith is that having done our duty we must be prepared to welcome whatever He may send—joy as well as sorrow, good luck as well as bad luck. He will be like King Janaka who, when informed that his capital was ablaze, only remarked that it was no concern of his.
>
> The secret of his resignation and equanimity, remarked Gandhiji, was that he was ever awake, never remiss in the performance of his duty. Having done his dudy, he would leave the rest to God.

And so a man of prayer will in the first place be spared mishaps by the ever merciful Providence, but if the mishaps do come, he will not bewail his fate nor lay the blame on God, but bear them with an undisturbed peace of mind and joyous resignation to His will.[27]

William James has quoted extensively in the chapters 4 and 5 entitled "The Religion of Healthy-Mindedness" in his famous work, "The Varieties of Religious Experience," to illustrate the point that faith works "miracles". Dr. James C. Coleman has given a prominent place to "a belief" in the fact that religious philosophy is 'indispensable to' "The Prevention of Abnormal Behaviour."[28] Dr. C. Jung has given his opinion on the point that faith in God saves a man from mental ruination.[29] In fact, it is possible to quote extensively on this subject that mental health is not only preserved but even enriched magnificently if one reposes complete faith in the Supreme. Radhakrishnan has rightly stated:

"Sensitive and informed minds believe that the fundamental need of the world, far deeper than any social, political or economic readjustment, is a spiritual reawakening, a recovery *of faith*."[30] His appreciation for the path of devotion is unmistakable.

"The principal centre of spiritual life is the heart. By inward prayer, we enable the heart to participate in the union with God. . . .By devotion and prayer we attain a state of mind in which we become detached from everything pertaining to the world and are directly united with God. Bhakti includes faith and love."[31]

Thus devotion is desirable from the standpoints of spiritual progress, social prosperity, and individual growth alike.

Let us not forget that in those periods when there were no newspapers, no radios, no television sets, and no widespread literacy even, the devotees spread the message of social cohesion and unity, individual sanity and cantentment, and brought the quintessence of the most profound knowledge to the door-steps of every man. The saints and devotees have left an indelible imprint of their constructive thought on the minds of the vast bulk of humanity and gave a new orientation to the thought, culture and literature of the people. As I have already stated, the present world is sitting on a volcano of destruction. There is only one way of easing the situation. "We must work for a world in which all races can blend and mingle, each retaining its special characteristics and developing whatever is best in it."[32] And only the persons of sterling and sincere devotion shall spontaneously endeavour to generate the forces of synthesis and unity. The value of devotion is, therefore, evident.

But what is meant by devotion or Bhakti? I shall not go into the details of the nature of Bhakti or devotion here. That would be found in the present work itself. But it may be stated that devotion signifies an intense love for God. According to Radhakrishnan "through it we offer our emotional possibilities to the divine . . . . If we do not love and worship, we become shut within the prison of our own egoism".[33] Devotion implies a firm attachment for the Lord and the consequent detachment from the mundane objects.[34] For a man of devotion the whole world of distinctions and selfishness is dead. For him everywhere God alone exists.[35] His entire life is dedicated to the Lord[36] And as he has completely surrendered himself to the Lord, he cannot be affected by any trace of worldliness.[37] The devotee pleases his Lord by a selfless devotion which means an attitude of complete and sincere dedication and the consequent alsolute attachment. The Lord cannot be pleased so much by anything else like sacrifice, knowledge etc. as by the self-less devotion.[38] Therefore, a devotee serves his Lord through speech, body, mind, and heart.[39]

Devotion provides a case of opening the gates of salvation for everybody and simplification and democratization of spiritual knowledge, through a process that is at once pleasant and charming.[40] Devotion is a region where the surging emotions, feelings and sentiments rush spontaneously to touch the feet of the Lord in a spirit of blissful dedication and fragrant self-surrender.

In my opinion devotion must be distinguished from the popular concept of religion. It should also be distinguished from philosophy Philosophy signifies an intellectual pursuit of the Ultimate Reality. The world is a puzzle and the philosopher tries to solve it through a logical study of Reality. A man thinks like Omar Khayyam and states :

"Into this Universe, and Why not knowing,
Nor Whence, like Water willy-nilly flowing;
And out of it, as Wind along the Waste,
I know not whither, willy-nilly blowing.

Strange, is it not ? that of the myriads who
Before us pass'd the door of Darkness through,
Not one returns to tell us of the Road,
Which to discover we must travel too."

Philosophy is an attempt to unravel these mysteries in its methodical and logical form. Philosophy is, therefore, shorn of feelings and adopts the path of rigid logic. Devotion, on the other hand, gives utmost importance to faith, to feelings. *Intellectualism* has its own shortcomings. It is the prisoner of its own limits. Faith, on the other hand, is not satisfied with an intellectual approach. A well-known description of faith is found in the Epistle to the Hebrews where it has been described as "the substance (or assurance) of things hoped for, the evidence (or proving) of things not seen."[41] But a better description of faith comes from Erich Fromm when he states : "Faith is certainty of conviction based on one's experience of thought and feeling, not assent to propositions on credit of the composer."[42] The entire life of a devotee is steeped in this faith. Like Santayana, a man of devotion would declare:

"O world, thou choosest not the better part.
It is not wisdom to be only wise,
And on the inward vision close the eyes,
But it is wisdom to believe the heart.
Columbus found a world, and had no chart,
Save one that faith deciphered in the skies;
To trust the soul's invincible surmise
Was all his science and his only art.
Our knowledge is a torch of smoky pine

That lights the pathway but one step ahead
Across a void of mystery and dread.
Bid, then, the tender light of faith to shine
By which alone the mortal heart is led
Unto the thinking of the thought divine."

If philosophy suffers from too much love for a rigid and *stony* logic, religion, at least in its popular form, has a tendency to become merely a faithful pursuit of scriptural rules, a sincere conformity to the prescribed rites and rituals. In its lofty form religion is a transformation of individual life in the light of the Supreme. Writing about this lofty form of religion U. Thithila has stated in his book "The Path of the Buddha":

"It means truth, that which really is. It also means law, the law which exists in a man's own heart and mind. It is the principle of righteousness.

Dhamma, this law of righteousness, exists not only in a man's heart and mind; it exists in the universe also. All the universe is an embodiment and revelation of dhamma. When the moon rises and sets, the rains come, the crops grow, the seasons change, it is because of dharma, for dharma is the law residing in the heart of the universe which makes matter act in the ways revealed by the studies of modern science in physics, chemistry, zoology, botany, and astronomy. Dhamma or dharma is the true nature of every existing thing, animate and inanimate."[43]

But, generally, religion has been understood and accepted in a restricted sense of following certain set formulae. That is why in the past, religion has provoked the religious wars and conflicts and has brought about destruction of human lives and ideals. Our present India is a standing example of the destruction that this 'popular' religion has brought about. That is why even now human beings are divided into Hindus and Muslims, Christians and Jews, Buddhists and Jains. Thus religion has a tendency of accepting a set line of conduct. But devotion, even though it too can have grades, cannot be satisfied with any conservative ideal. It sets before it the Lord Himself and does not need the intervention or interpretation of any intermediary agency like a clergy, or a maulavi or a purohita. Therefore, a man of devotion defies the popular religion and opposes any act that wrongs others and kindles the fire of universal brotherhood.[44]

Nāmadeva states:

"Vows, fasts, and austerities are not at all necessary; nor is it necessary for you to go on a pilgrimage. Be you watchful in your hearts and always sing the name of Hari. It is not necessary to give up eating food or drinking water; fix your mind on the feet of Hari. Yoga or sacrificial ceremonies or giving up objects of desire is not wanted. Realize a fondness for the feet of Hari."[45]

Kabīra observes:

"I shut not my eyes, I close not my ears, I do not mortify my body;
I see with eyes open and smile, and behold His beauty everywhere.
Whatever I do, it becomes His worship.
All I achieve is His service."[46]

Tirunavukkarasu, a devotee from South India, sings:

"Thou to me art parents, Lord
Thou all kinsmen that I need,
Thou to me art loved one fair,
Thou art treasure rich indeed.
Family, friends, home art Thou,
Life and joy I draw from Thee,
False world's good by Thee, I leave,
Gold, pearl, wealth art Thou to me."[47]

Jafara, a Muslim devotee and poet, has put the matter very effectively by stating:

"I did not see that divine light in the mosques and the temples. I saw it only in the temple of my heart."[48]

The basic craving of a devotee's heart has been eloquently expressed by Mīrā by saying: "Mere to Giridhara Gopāla, dūsaro na koi" (Only Giridhara Gopāla is mine. I consider none else to be mine.)

The Gopīs of the Bhāgavata, in the true spirit of a sincere devotee, declared: "Lord, You alone are the friend, soul, and the dearest being for all the embodied beings."[49]

Thus devotion is an attitude which is, to a great extent, distinct from philosophy and religion.

It may be mentioned here that some persons have tried to show that Bhakti or devotion is not Indian in its original form. Devotion is a plant brought from outside India.

Burnell[50], Weber[51], Caldwell[52], Hopkins[53], Bhandarkar[54], Grierson[55] are the prominent scholars who are of the opinion that the rise of devotion in India was inspired by the influence of Christianity. On the other hand scholars like Fawcett[56], Barth[57], Tarachand[58], and Humayun Kabir[59] express the opinion that Islamic influence was responsible for the rise of devotion in India.

In my opinion both these views are quite untenable. I have established in the present work that bhakti or devotion is purely Indian in origin and its traces are present even in the Ṛgveda and the Unanisads.

Barnett[60], Macnicoll[61], Estlin Carpenter[62a] and many other scholars too have come out with the view that bhakti or devotion cannot be considered an imported concept in any case. I am sure that no wise person shall dispute the fact that bhakti is an Indian product, after carefully going through the clear evidence available on the point. Dr. Ashirbadilal Shrivastava's following observations, therefore, should be found readily acceptable :
"It will, thus, be seen that the movement (of Bhakti) was not altogether new, and that it did not owe its origin to Islam, as has been erroneously supposed by some modern writers."[62b]

Let us, therefore, take it for granted that Bhakti is certainly an out and out growth.

That Bhakti has played a very important role in Indian life cannot be disputed by any judicious reader of Indian history. Indian art, culture, literature practically everything has been influenced by the cult of devotion. I am sure that the Bhagavadgītā and the Bhāgavata have played a dominant and important role in moulding the thoughts of the scholars as well as the common man in the direction of devotion, Even Śaṁkara,

Rāmānuja, and Vallabha, the most prominent Ācāryas of the Vedāntic school of philosophical thought, were influenced not only by the Bhagavadgīta but also by the Bhāgavata Purāṇa. While there is no dispute as to the influence of the Bhagavadgīta, some people may express some doubt as to the influence exercised by the Bhāgavata on the Ācāryas. But there is no justifiable ground for doubting suce an influence of the Bhāgavata. Let us not forget that the Bhāgavata is an old work. I have already established in my work, The Synthetic Philosophy of the Bhāgavata, (which won the degree of Ph. D. under its changed title, The Concepts of Īśvara, Prakṛti, and Jīva in the Bhāgavata Purāṇa. for me from Agra University) that the Bhāgavata is a very old work and that it was composed much earlier than the birth of Christ even.

Madhva has stated in his work Bhāgavata-tātparya-nirṇaya that Śaṁkara had written some commentary on the Bhāgavata. Though that commentary is not available at present, yet there is no reason why we should doubt the statement of Madhva. It is significant to note that Śaṁkara has taken the care of not disputing the basic creed of the Bhāgavatas even in his commentary on the Bramha Sūtras. He writes :

> "Concerning this system we remark that we do not intend to controvert the doctrine that Nārāyaṇa, who is higher than the Undeveloped, who is the highest Self, and the Self of all, reveals Himself by dividing Himself in multiple ways; for various scriptural passages, such as 'He is one fold, He is three-fold' teach us that the highest Self appears in manifold forms. Nor do we mean to object to the inculcation of unceasing concentration of mind in the highest Being which appears in the Bhāgavata doctrine under the forms of reverential approach, etc.; for that we are to meditate on the Lord we know full well from Smṛti and Scripture."[62c]

This expression of reverence for faith was no doubt inspired by the study of the Bhāgavata. Śaṁkara has even taken a piece from the Bhāgavata literally and quoted it as the statement of Vyāsa himself.[63] Then, there are other evidences found in the works of Śaṁkara which lead us to the conclusion that the Bhāgavata certainly influenced the mind of this great

Ācārya of the Vedāntic school.[64] The influence of the Bhāgavata is also evident in the writings of two other Ācāryas of the Vedāntas *viz.* Rāmānuja and Vallabha. I have dealt with the question of the influence of the Bhāgavata on these three Ācāryas in the present work at appropriate occasions. So far as the concepts of Bhakti or devotion of the three Ācāryas are concerned, they have been duly explained in the present work. A reader who has read only the conflicting expositions of the Brahma Sūtras by Śaṁkara, Rāmānuja, and Vallabha shall have a pleasant surprise in store when he goes through the bhakti literature of the three Ācāryas. When Śaṁkara prescribes a devotion of Śrīkṛṣṇa for cleansing the heart and mind[65] and sees his Brahman in the Lord of Yadus[66] and prays for the vision of Śrīkṛṣṇa[67], he comes so close to Rāmānuja who begins his Vedānta-Sārah with the following adoration of Viṣṇu (who is nondistinct from Śrīkṛṣṇa):

> "I bow unto Viṣṇu, who has as his body all the sentient and non-sentient beings, who is the self of all objects, who is associated with Śrī and who is the ocean of bliss untaint-with impurity."[68]

and asserts "that only meditation of the form of bhakti leads to the attainment of Brahman"[69]
and to Vallabha who states : "The Lord of Vrja is to be served and worshipped in every way heartily."[70] and adds: "There is no God other than Śrīkṛṣṇa."[71]

The reader is bound to be struck by this unanimity. If not for anything else, at least due to this unifying and synthesizing power, the path of bhakti, devotion, becomes adorable. I am grateful to God for giving me an opportunity for writing on such a sublime subject. I have tried to present the concept of bhakti in all its facets and dimensions. I am sure a perusal of the present work shall be able to impress the desirability of devotion upon the minds of all.

Let me confess that though I have sincerely tried to do justice with the subject, yet the subject is so ponderous that it is just possible that the learned readers may detect certain error here and there. I, however, pray them to be charitable and magnanimous in their assessment of the merits of the work, both due to the loftiness of the subject, and erring nature of a human being. Success of every good attempt is in fact grateful to bountiful nature of the good and the worthy. So far as I myself am concerned, I have experienced a rare sense of satisfaction by writing on Bhakti, devotion, which, like the story of Rāmāyaṇa, to quote the words of Bhavabhūti, "purifies a person from his sins, brings about welfare to him and contributes to the well-being of one and all like a mother and the Ganges."[72]

Yes, it is my firm belief that the present state of the individual and social lives can be set right only by persons who drink deep at the fountain of devotion. T.S. Eliot has very effectively portrayed the present plight of people in his poem "The Rock":

"The Word of the Lord come unto me, saying;
O miserable cities of designing men,
O wretched generation of enlightened men,
Betrayed in the mazes of your ingenuities,
Sold by the proceeds of your proper inventions,
I have given you hands which you turn from worship,
....
I have given you lips, to express friendly sentiments,
....
Much is your reading but not the Word of God,
Much is your building, but not the House of God,
..........."[73]

And W.B. Yeats, too, has tried to present the situation in a similar vein when he states:

"Things fall apart: the centre cannot hold
Mere anarchy is loosed upon the world,
The blood-dimmed tide is loosed, and everywhere,
The ceremony of innocence is drowned:
The best lack all conviction, while the worst are full of passionate intensity."[74]

We need persons of sterling devotion to change this scene of disgust and degradation. History bears a testimony to this fact that whenever society sufferred from abnormal agonies and moral degenerations, persons of devotion came forward to save the situation and pave the way of the progress of humanity. The lives and contributions of Tulasīdāsa, Kabīra, Nāmadeva, Caitanya, Mīrā, Narasiṁha Mehatā etc. corroborate this fact. Once again when people are marching towards the nadir of degeneration, the devotees can improve the situation. They can bring about not only spiritual resurrection of humanity, but can also bring a sense of sanity and happiness in the lives of countless people and pave the path of social health and prosperity. Protagoras had declared. "Man is the Measure of all things." Walt Whitman has written in his poem 'The Base of All Metaphysics':

"Having studied the new and antique, the Greek and Germanic systems,
Kant having studied and stated, Fichte and Schelling and Hegel,
Stated the lore of Plato, and Socrates greater than Plato,
And greater than Socrates sought and stated, Christ divine having studied long,
I see reminiscent to-day those Greek and Germanic systems,
See the philosophies all, Christian churches and tenets see,
Yet underneath Socrates clearly see, and underneath Christ the divine I see,
The dear love of man for his comrade, the attraction of friend to friend,
Of the well-married husband and wife, of children and parents.
Of city for city and land for land."

Yes, this peaceful environment, this affection for humanity can be generated through an attitude of candid devotion to the Lord. Mahatma Gandhi, who was devotion incarnate, has rightly pointed out :

"There is an eternal struggle raging in man's breast between the powers of darkness and of light, and he, who has not the sheet-anchor of prayer to rely upon, will be a victim to the powers of darkness.

"The man of prayer will be at peace with himself and with the whole world, the man who goes about the affairs of the world without a prayerful heart will be miserable and will make the world also miserable."[75]

Let us not forget that India, no the world, is more indebted to the works like the Bhagavadgītā, the Bhāgavata, etc. which have glorified faith and devotion than to any abstruse work of knowledge; it is more indebted to persons of sterling devotion, like Tulasīdāsa, Nānaka, Kabīra, Mīrā, Gandhi etc. than to any pedant. Devotion is that torch that lights the world and the pathway of real spirituality alike.

Devotion implies a transformation of one's life in the light of one's faith, one's love for the Lord. And when one's life becomes imbued with the hearty love for one's Lord, one leads a life that can be an envy of any man of knowledge and an examplar for any lover of humanity.

Bhakti is as old as humanity. One cannot be expected to add anything 'original' to expound its concept. And yet something added can be called original in the following words of Dr. Raju :

"Many in India have little respect for new arguments. The undertaking to discover them may be dishonest, if not childish. What the philosopher has to do is to trace out certain generalities in the intricate web of experience. Much depends on the way he marshals our experience, on the point with which he starts, and the way he proceeds. Thereby he may see some new significance in our experience, not noticed by others. Novelty, therefore, does not mean that the philosopher will not be an advaitin, a dvaitin, etc., but some new one. This misconception about originality in philosophy, prevalent among some in India, has to be cleared. Originality lies in the discovery of a new method of approach to our problems, and also in the application of some methods or principles to some new problems."[76]

Our present approach to devotion, therefore, can be called in this sense original. In fact every approach containing logical elements has some novelty.

But novelty is always a relative term. For some devotion implies perpetual duality. For others, this may not be the case. On my part, I am convinced that real devotion always leads a devotee from the realm of duality to the domain of throbbing unity. A real devotee, like the Gopikas of the Bhāgavata, becomes just an image of his Lord.[77]

References

1. My works are:
"Peace, Philosophy, And "Progress" dedicated to the memory of the late Pandit Jawaharlal Nehru, and containing a Foreword by Prof. Humayun Kabir; "Essentials of Psychology"; "Education And Human Society"; Horizon of Human Progress"; "Humanitarian Ethics"; "The Universalistic Thought of India"; The Synthetic Philosophy of the Bhāgavata"; "The Nondualistic Trends of Bhakti Philosophy"
My Hindi works are "Samāja Darsana", "Svastha Mana, Svastha Tana, Svastha Jīvana", and "Naye Kshitija".
2. codanālakṣaṇo 'rtho dharmah.—Jaimini 1-1-2.
āmnāyasya kriyārthatvāt.—Mimāṁsā Sūtra, 1-2-1.
3. kṣurasya dhārā niśitā duratyayā durgaṁ pathastat kavayo vadanti.—Kaṭha Upaniṣad 1-3-14.
vide Bhagavadgītā, 12.5 : Bhāgavata, 10.14-4.
4. Nārada Bhakti Sūtra, 58 : anyasmāt saulbhyaṁ bhaktau Bhagavadgītā, 18-66; Bhāgavata, 11-14-20.
5. Bhā. 10-29-15.
6. Hari Mohan Bhattacharya, The Principles of Philosophy, University of Calcutta, 1948, p. 328.
7. jānāmi dharmaṁ na ca me pravṛttiḥ.
jānāmi adhramaṁ na ca me nivṛttiḥ.
8. Philosophic Problems, editied by Maurice etc., Macmillan Co., New York, p. 638.
9. Prabodha Sudhākara, verse 200.
10. Vedānta Sāra, p. 1.
11. Kṛṣṇāśraya, verse 9
12. Antaḥkaraṇa-prabodha, verse 1.
13. Viveka Cūḍāmaṇi, verses 18 to 29.

14. Brahma-jñānāvalī-mālā, verse 20; Ātmabodhaḥ, verse 48. Brahmānucintanam, verse 28; Prauḍhānubhūtih, verse 3.
15. Bhā. 10-44-15.
yat yat karma karomi tat tadakhilaṁ śaṁbho tavārādhanaṁ Saṁkara's Parā Pūjā, verse 10.
16. Bhā. 8-1-10.
17. Bhā. 10-30-3.
18. vyādhasyācaraṇaṁ dhruvasya ca vayo vidyā gajendrasya kā kubjāyaḥ kimu nāma rupamadhikaṁ kintat sudanaṁdhanaṁ; vaṁśaḥ ko vidurasya yādavapaterugrasya kim pauruṣaṁ bhaktyā tuṣyati kevalaṁ na ca guṇairbhaktipriyo mādhavaḥ.
19. Bhā. 10-42-1: rasapradaḥ.
20. Bhā. 10-47-25:munīnāmapi durlabhā.
21. Bṛhadāraṇyaka Upaniṣad 2-4-14: vijñātāramare kena vijaniyāt.
22. Bhā. 11-14-20.
"At the heart of any philosophy worth the name is vision"—Dr. Waismann.
vide "English Philosophy Since 1900", by G.J. Warnock, Oxford University Press, New York, 1958, p. 164.
"Ramahi kevala prema piyārā
Jāni leu jo jānanihārā."—Tulasīdāsa.
23. Bhā. 7-9-44.
24. Tagore's Gitāñjali, no. 77.
25. Bhā. 9-21-2.
"Parahita sarisa dharma nahi bhāi"—Tulasīdāsa.
26 Bhā. 11-20-17.
27. Ramanama-The Infallible Remedy, by Mahatma Gandhi, Edited and published by Anand T. Hingorani, Karachi 1947, p. 85-86.
28. An Outline of Abnormal Psychology, edited by Garner Murphy and Arthur J. Bachrach, The Modern Library, New York, revised edition, p.535.
29. "I therefore consider the religious teaching of a life hereafter consonant with the standpoint of psychic hygiene."—
Modern Man in search of a soul, by Jung, C.G., New York, Harcourt, 1933, p. 129.
"Thus faith whether in oneself or in other men or in God means a realistic assessment of the powers and helps within our reach and a helpful dependence on them towards the full realization of the hidden possibilities of man. By faith in oneself one is able to restore balance in a disintegrated personality and make the best of one's capacities. By faith in others we expand our personality into society and attain the full evolution of our faculties in an intimate communion with our fellow beings. By faith in God we rise above

the temporal and limiting world to a vision of our eternal and divine goal and hope to attain it by an intimate communion with the Godhead. Thus faith works a real miracle in human life and raises it to heights unimaginable by our external view of things."—The Art of Living, edited by Dr. Prem Nath, University Publishers, Delhi, 1963, p. 188.

30. Recovery of Faith, George Allen & Unwin Ltd., London, 1956 p. 1.
31. Ibid, p. 162.
32. The Hindu View of Life, by Radhakrishnan, Unwin Books, 1960 p. 76.
33. Indian Philosophy, Vol. I, 1929, p. 558.
34. "sā parānuraktirīśvare" (Śāṇḍilya Bhakti S.-2)
"sā tvasmin parama premarūpā" (Nārada Bhakti S.2)
"bhaktirasya bhajanaṁ etādihamutropādhinairāśyenāmuṣmina manaḥ kalpatam" (Gopāla Pūrvatāpani Upaniṣad, 2-1)
"manogatiravicchinnā harau premapariplutā, abhisaṁdhivinirmuktā bhaktirviṣṇuvaśaṁkatī" (Nārada Pāñcarāta)
"Prema gali ati sāṁkarī tā mai do da samāya"
(The lane of love is so excessively small that it cannot contain two).
35. "jita dekhun tita syāmamayī hai"
(wherever I look, I find the Lord)
Bhā 3-9-6
36. Bhā. 11-2-36.
37. Bhā. 11-14-18: 10-14-58.
38. Bhā. 7-7-51, 52.
39. Bhā. 10-80-3.
40. Bhā. 7-6-23; 10-32-2; 10-72-6; 11-1-6; 11-7-18.
41. Faith And Reason in Religion, by George Galloway, Nisbet & Co. Ltd., London, 1927, p. 25.
42. Philosophy of Religion, edited by George G.L. Abernethy and T.A. Langford, The Macmillan Company, New York, 1962, p. 60.
43. Quoted from "Samāja Darśana" written by the author, and published by Sahitya Sadhana Mandira, p. 112.
44. Bhagavadgītā 12-13 to 20.
45. Influence of Islam on Indian Culture, by Dr. Tarachand, Indian Press (Publications) Private Ltd., Allahabad, 1963 p. 223.
46. Ibid, p. 164.
47. Ibid, p. 89.
48. Na dekhā vaha kahin jalavā, jo dekhā khānae dila men Bahuta masjida men sara mārā, bahuta-sā ḍhūṇḍhā butakdānā.

49. Bhā. 10-29-32.

50. Indian Antiquary, vol. III, p. 308; Vol. IV, p. 183.

51. Indian Antiquary, Vol. III, pp. 22, 47.

52. A Comparative Grammar of the Dravidian Languages.

53. India Old and New.

54 Vaiṣṇavism and Śaivism.

55. Journal of the Royal Asiatic Society, 1907, pp. 311-36.

56. Anthropology, Bulletin, vol. III, No. 1. editied by Thurson.

57. Religions of India.

58. Influence of Islam on Indian Culture, 107.

59. Our Heritage.

60. Heart of India, Bhagavadgītā etc.

61. Indian Theism, Appendix C.

62. (a) Theism in Medieval India; Note on Christianity in India.

(b) Medieval Indian Culture, published by Shiva Lal Agarwal & Co. (P) Ltd., Agra, 1264, p. 63.

(c) Śaṁkara's commentary on Brama-sutra 2-2-42. vide The Vedānta-Sūtras with the commentary by Śaṁkarācārya, translated by George Thibaut, The Sacred Books of The East, edited by F. Max Muller, vol. XXXIV, published from Oxfrod at The Clarendon Press, 1890, p. 440-441.

63. Compare the verse no. 222 of Saṁkara's Probodha Sudhākara with the Bhāgavata 10-30-15.

64. vide "Influence of Bhāgavata" in Chapter IV of present work.

65. Saṁkara's Prabodha Sudhākara, verse 167.

66. ibid, verse 200.

67. Kṛṣṇāṣṭakam, verse 1, Minor Works of Śaī Śaṅkrācārya edited by H.R. Bhagavata, Oriental Book Agency, Poona, p. 391.

68. Vedāntasāra edited by V. Krishnamacharaya, The Adyar Library, 1933, p. 1.

69. Vedanta Saṁgraha, para 128, Sri Ramakrishna Ashrama, Mysore 1956, p. 100.

70. Catuśloki, verse 1; Bṛhatstotrasaritsāgarasya, Dvittīyo Baāgah, Published by Jyeṣṭhārāma Sharma, and printed at Native Opinion Printing Press, Bombay, Śālivāhana Śaka 1827, p. 47.

71. Aṅtaḥkaraṅa Parabodha v. 1, ibid, page 42.

72. pāpabhyaśca punāti vardhayati ca
śreyāṁsi seyaṁ kathā
māṅgalyā ca manoharā ca
jagato māteva gaṅgeva ca.

vide Uttara-Rāma-Caritaṁ by D. Lala Ramāyadupāla Singh, Śāradā Pustaka Bhavana, Allahabad, 1965, p. 362.

73. T.S. Eliot, Symposium, Publishers, Frank & Cass Co. Ltd., London, 1995, p. 198.

74. W.B. Yeats, Collected Poems (1937)—'The Second Coming'.

75. 'God is Truth'. Bharatiya Vidya Bhavan, Bombay.

76. P.T. Raju, Idealistic Thought of India, George Allen & Unwin Ltd., London, 1953, pp. 26-27.

77. Bhā. 10-30-3: priyasya pratirūḍhamūrtayaḥ.

2

An Account of the Rise of Bhakti

"Human minds do not throw up sudden stray thoughts without precedents or ancestors : History is continuity and advance. There is no such thing as utterly spontaneous generation. . . .Tradition links generation with one another and all progress is animated by ideas which it seems to supersede. The debt we owe to our spiritual ancestors is to study them. Traditional continuity is not mechanical reproduction; it is creative transformation, an increasing approximation to the ideal of truth. . . .The main thing is to remember and create anew. Confucius said: "He who by reanimating the Old can gain knowledge of the New is fit to be a teacher."

—Radhakrishnan in
'Fragments of A Confession'
The Philosophy of Sarvapalli
Radhakrishnan, edited by
P.A. Schilpp.

"I have seen the ancient way, the old road that was taken by the former awakened beings and that is the path I follow."

—The Buddha in
Samyutta Nikaya, II, 106

. . . .

There is sometimes a tendency to assert that Bhakti or devotion has come to India from outside. Nothing can be further from truth. It was first Sir George Grierson, a noted orientalist, who expressed an opinion that Bhakti is a foreign element and that it has been introduced in India by the followers of the Christ from Europe who settled down in India to propagate their religion. Perhaps the underlying feeling behind this opinion was that everything that is good has come to India from the West, from where the British Masters had come to rule over the destinies of this nation after the overthrow of the Islamic power. This opinion gave birth to other writers who tried to plead that either devotion has come from the European Christians or from the Islamic preachers. In no case it is a product of India.

However, this opinion is wholly untenable and unwarranted. This becomes clear if we care to study the ancient literature called the Vedas, the Upanishads, the Purana or the epics. In fact the nature of Bhakti cannot be understood unless, we look to its fountainhead, the Vedic and epic literature. And the Vedic literature was composed much earlier than the European and the Islamic literatures. Hence, if we are to determine the original source of devotion, then it is the Vedic and Epic literature of India. Perhaps original Indian thought went as far as the West in the past and as the Western scholar is aware of his own literature, he pleaded that devotion has come to India from the West. We find that the terms Bhakti (devotion), Bhakta (devotee), and Bhajamahe (I worship Thee) have been used in the sense in which they are used at present even in the period of the ancient Vedas.

Bhakti : tasyate bhaktivansah syama(Atharva, 6-79-3)

Bhakta : Bhaktamabhaktamavyanto araja agnayovyanto ajarah (Ṛgveda 1-127-5)

Bhajamahe : mahastevisnosumatim bhajamahe (Ṛgveda, 1-156-3)

Bhajante : barhisado ye svadhaya sutasya bhajanta pitvasta ihagamistaah (Yajurveda. 19/56)

Not only this, we find the nine kinds of Bhakti that were elaborated later on in the Bhāgavata Puraṇa present in the Vedic literature.

The seer of the Ṛgveda declares: "Thy (God's) friendship is tasty and Thy attachment too is sweet." On other occasion he exclaims "You are ours, and we are yours" or "O you the Saviour, protector . . . you are our true mother and father." "We pray to Thee O dearest of dears."

Even in the Upanishads which are the works of knowledge, we find the sparks of devotion. For example, the Kena states "The Brahman is to be served and worshipped.", and Katha declares "This Self cannot be realized through preaching, intelligence or much learning; It can be realized only through the grace of God." The Svetasvatara proclaims "I come to Thy shelter with a desire of salvation." The Isa Upanishad prays Agni: "O Agni, Thou knowest all our deeds; dost Thou therefore lead us along the right path for our welfare; dost Thou guard us against sinful wrong paths. We pay our best homage and respect to Thee."

Iśa, Katha, Taittirīya, Chandogya, Brhadāranyaka, and the Śvetāśvatara are the prominent Upanishads which present to us some of the best examples of eulogy (stuti). Even salutation (Vandana) is found in them. Adoration (Arcanā) is present in the Bṛhadāraṇyaka. Even the spirit of self-surrender (ātmanivedana) which is the culmination of devotional feeling is present in the Śvetāśvatara when it writes: "I seek Thy shelter for salvation."

It should not be forgotten that faith (śraddhā) which is the basic element of devotion is present in the Vedic and the Upanishadic literatures. Śraddhā is the mother of the whole world of rites as Mantra is the father." The Śvetāśvatara goes to the extent of preaching Bhakti not only for the Lord, but even for the preceptor. It is very clear in declaring that self-realization is impossible without the divine grace. It states "Desirous of self-emancipation I take refuge under that Lord Who creates Brahmā in the beginning, hands over the Vedas to him, and enlightens our mind.

Prof. R.G. Bhandarkar rightly observes in his work 'Vaiṣṇavism, Śaivism And Other Minor Sects of Hindu Religion': "The description of the Godhead and the final pure serenity are instinct with the glow of love and admiration, and the treatise ends with an expression of self-surrender to the god who makes himself manifest in one's own intelligence. The Śve. Upanishad, therefore, stands at the door of the Bhakti-school and pours its loving adoration on Rudra-Śiva instead of on Vāuseva-Kṛṣṇa, as the Bhagavadgītā did in later times when the Bhakti doctrine was in full swing."

Even in the Brahma-sūtras of Bādarāyaṇa, which are strictly concerned with the way of knowledge, we find some mention of Bhakti. As a matter of fact 'upāsanā' which is found both in the Upanishads and the Brahma-sūtras imply devotion. But apart from this wide reference to 'upāsanā', clear reference to Bhakti is found in the third Adhyāya of the Brahma-sūtras, where it has been referred to as 'abhidhyāna' and 'saṁrādhana'.

The celebrated work, the Bhagavadgītā, which is an important part of the Mahābhārata gives due importance to Bhakti. In fact it declares that the Lord can be realized only through devotion. It also narrates the marks of a devotee . . . devotee is free from any trace of envy, selfishness, ego, mental disturbance, enmity, etc. The Gītā is an important work on devotion. It gives an analysis of the different kinds of devotees viz. Ārta, jijñāsu, Arthārthī and Jnānī. But the most dear kind of devotee to the Lord is a prema Bhakta or the devotee who loves his Lord just because he loves Him.

The Hindu religion is śruti-smṛti-purāṇokta i.e. it is in accordance with the tenets of the Vedas, Smṛti literature and the Puraṇas. We have already seen that Bhakti is found in the Vedic literature. It is also found in the Bhagavadgītā, which is supposed to be the most prominent Smṛti. Now we can proceed to find out if the Purāṇas, which enjoy the topmost popularity in the Hindu religion, too preach the gospel of devotion.

There are eighteen major Purāṇas in Hinduism. All of them accept devotion as the best way of getting liberation. The Viṣṇu, the Bhāgavata, the Nāradīya, the Brahmavaivarta, the Vāmana, the Varāha, the Kūrma (these are called the Vaiṣṇava Purāṇas), the Vāyu, the Śiva, the Skanda, and the Linga (these are called the Śaiva Purāṇas) give utmost importance to devotion.

The Bhāgavata declares that Bhakti is higher than even Mukti (salvation). It declares that charities, vows, penances, sacrifices, recitations of prayers, studies, self-restraints and such other manifold good thihgs are all meant for acquiring the Bhakti of the Lord. That indeed is the highest religion of man, from which is acquired unselfish and uninterrupted Bhakti of the Lord.

The Bhakti has been conceived by the Bhāgavata in two ways. One is the Primary Bhakti, which has been termed as Parā, Phala or the Paramā Bhakti, and has been considered the highest fruit or achievement of human life; the other is secondary Bhakti, which has been termed parā or Sādhana Bhakti and is considered as the destroyer of sins and the begetter of salvation. Naturally, the Bhāgavata attaches supreme importance to Parā Bhakti.

The Viṣṇu Purāṇa too attaches foremost importance to Bhakti. It talks about the pure or avyabhicāriṇī Bhakti. It helps a person in seeking union with the supreme Truth. The Viṣṇu Purāṇa observes "Meditating on the Lord as not different from his own self, Prahlāda became absorbed in Him and took himself to be the Lord Himself. He forgot his individual self and knew nothing except that he himself was the imperishable and the limitness Parmatman."

Even the great preacher of the Advaita, Sañkara, in his work Prabodhasudhākara, states : "Vairāgya (dispassion), ātmabodha (knowledge) and Bhakti (devotion)—these three are the means of mukti (salvation)." In that very work he adds: "The control of breath, good company, the renunciation of mental propensities and devotion to the fact of Lord Hari soon effect the control of the mind. "But even out of these the indispensible factor is Bhakti. Śaṅkara accepts this in that work by writing "The internal organ i.e. the mind is never purified in the absence of Bhakti of Lord Kṛṣṇa; it is washed off its sins (and becomes pure) by means of Bhakti, just as clothes by soda-water."

Madhva is emphatic that without knowledge devotion is not possible, and without devotion knowledge is not possible." God becomes pleased with devotion. Vallabha declares that Kṛṣṇa is the only God devoid of every blemish. Caitanya was himself an exemplary devotee. He recited the name Kṛṣṇa day and night.

Kabīra, a gerat saint, says that he is a dog wearing rope of Rāma in his neck and standing at the door of Rāma. He is of the opinion that the only worthwhile thing in the world is love of God. Lord Rāma is his husband. Nānaka, the founder of Sikhism, was a great devotee. The best work is to recite the name of Rama, preached Nānaka.

Narasī, who was a popular devotee of Gujarat, states: Saints, we are the traders of names of Rāma alone."

Tulasīdāsa, who is the most noteworthy poet of Hindi, gave devotion supreme importance. His classic works Rāma-carita-mānasa and Vinaya-Patrikā are clear examples of it. According to him, a person with devotion is like a tank or river without water. A person's merits are useless in the absence of devotion just as dishes are uselss without salt. Ramakrishna Paramahansa, Aurbindo, Gandhi, in fact every great Indian is a person of devotion. Gandhi declared "Ramanāma is my infallible help."

come directly under control of the mind. What even out of these the [illegible] factor is Bhakti. Bhakti [illegible] [illegible] by virtue. The [illegible] never [illegible] Bhakti. [illegible] is washed off [illegible] by means of Bhakti just as clothes by cold water.

[illegible] that Bhakti is [illegible] and without [illegible] knowledge [illegible] impossible. [illegible] declares that [illegible] devoted [illegible] himself [illegible] Krishnaswarupa [illegible]

[illegible] great [illegible] standing at the door of Rama. He is of the opinion that the only worthy thing in the world is love of Lord Rama [illegible] her husband [illegible] the foundation [illegible] was a great devotee. The best [illegible] Krishna.

[illegible] who was [illegible] popular [illegible] Saints are the [illegible]

Tulsidas who is the most [illegible] poet of Hindi, [illegible] supreme importance [illegible] are clear examples of it. According to him, a person with devotion is like a [illegible] without [illegible] are useless [illegible] devotion [illegible] Gandhi, in fact, every [illegible] devotion. Gandhiji declared "Ramanama is my [illegible]"

3

Bhakti and the Bhāgavata

Animittā bhāgavatī bhaktiḥ siddhergarīyasī

—Bhā. 3-25-33

Na sādhayati māṁ yogo na sāṁkhyaṁ dharma uddhava

na svādhyāyastapo tyāgo yathā bhaktirmamorjitā.

—Bhā. 11-14-20

Muktiṁ dadātī karhicitsma na bhaktiyogam.

—Bhā. 5-6-18

Na tapobhirna vedaiśca na jñānenāpi karmaṇā

harirhi sādhyate bhaktyā pramāṇaṁ tatra gopikāḥ.

—Bhāgavatamāhātmya, 2-18

Padma Purāṇa.

The Bhāgavata occupies a very important position in the realm of Indian philosophy, religion, and culture. I have already discussed the questions of the importance of the Bhāgavata as well the period of its composition in my book "The Synthetic Philosophy of the Bhāgavata", which is merely the name of my thesis for the degree of Ph.D., its original name being "The Concepts of Īśvara, Prakṛti. and Jīva in the Bhāgavata Purāṇa."[1] Since these topics have been discussed there at great length, it would be redundant to repeat the same here. Nor is it desirable for our purposes to repeat the same thing here. Our sole object at present is to study the concept of bhakti as delineated by the Bhāgavata and to find out how far this concept has influenced the great thinkers of Indian Philosophy.

That the Bhāgavata Purāṇa is one of the most popular works of Indian literature cannot be disputed. The very fact that there are eighty-one commentaries in Sanskrit alone on this work, and in Bengali alone some forty translations of this work are available, besides its translation in practically every language of India[2] and in French, Persian and English languages gives an impression to every reader that the Bhāgavata must be quite popular.

The secret of this popularity of the Bhāgavata lies in its literary qualities, and the importance it attaches to the method of bhakti as a means of attaining the Supreme Truth. It has placed before human beings a god who is the beautifier of the beauty itself, besides being an examplar of superhuman strength, virtues, magnanimity, kindness, and everything that a human heart wants to see in his deity.

The Bhāgavata is a great work that tries to prepare the minds of common men for the ultimate realization of the Supreme through the initial stages of devotion and dedication.

The Bhāgavata has pointed to the Ultimate Truth by stating that prior to the creation only that Truth existed. There was neither Sat nor Asat present at that period.[3] That Supreme Truth has been described as beginningless, attributeless, eternal, nondual.[4] This very Supreme Truth has been described as Brahman, Paramātmā (Supreme Soul), and Bhagavān (God) by the learned.[5] Brahman is the name given to this Supreme Truth by the Upanishads and the followers of the path of knowledge. The followers of the Yoga Mārga call it as Paramātmā or Īśvara. And the believers in bhakti call it as Bhāgavān.[6] The Supreme is pure knowledge and single and is called Vāsudeva by the learned.[7] He is Knowledge alone.[8]

But the Bhāgavata is quite aware of the fact that the people have different types of likings. Therefore they try to understand and interpret this Supreme in accordance with their aptitudes and liking, tendency and choice.[9] But the man of knowledge does not forget the ultimate nature of the Truth and realizes this fact that the Supreme has many names and forms.[10]

The Bhāgavata has a firm grasp of human psychology. It is not advisable to forget that a man is a bundle of instincts and impulses, desires and aspirations. They bind him to the earth. They do not allow him to rise to the region of the Supreme Truth. The path of knowledge is a way of suffering.[11] How, after all, an ordinary man can be convinced that he should concentrate his attention on the Supreme devoid of any shape or form? Who can know that Supreme?[12] Human intelligence and eyes cannot reach Him.[13] Therefore, the wise seers stop from using any words to describe Him.[14]

Therefore, some other device that shall do justice with the natural tendencies of a man, a common man, has to be found out. There should be some way whereby the natural impulses shall be directed towards the Supreme rather automatically. There should be some method whereby the instincts and impulses shall be spiritualized. After all human mind has to be led to the Supreme by and by. Any worship that demands an eradication of the structure of natural tendencies of a man.

cannot be liked or appreciated by a common man. One may call him a fool, an ignorant person who shall be required to undertake repeated births and suffer a number of agonies and pangs due to his attachment to the mundane objects. But that would not help the matter. That would not change the common man. That would not transform his heart and mind. Let us, therefore, in the interest of the Supreme Truth, and the well-being of the common men, devise a new path that shall tame the impulses, transform the natural urges, and change the life of the common man. This new path is the path of devotion. This path is not new in the sense that it has not been invented by the Bhāgavata. It is new in the the sense that, for the first time, that emphasis which must be given to it, was given by the Bhāgavata. And at the same time the ultimate cause of the Supreme Truth was not ignored or compromised. The Nirguṇa, the Supreme devoid of attributes, Himself was sought through this new path; for ultimately all the paths of worship reach Him alone.[15] After all the Saguṇa is not different from the Nirguṇa.[16] The indeterminate, infinite Brahman alone becomes the Saguṇa for the pleasure of the devotees and those who are not yet competent to walk on the straight and narrow path of knowledge, much like is a rain-bow without a string.[17]

How pleasant and beautiful is a rainbow which pervades the whole sky as it fills the heart of a spectator with pleasure and an inner satisfaction. But from where does this rainbow appear? It appears from the sky itself and it is lost in the sky itself after some time. It merely acts as a means of attracting the hearts and minds of the spectators towards the vast, unfathomable, blue sky. Brahman is much like this great sky, infinite, endless, beginningless, imperceptible, defier of any description. The Saguṇa is only the perceptible, creation of the infinite Brahman. Just as a rainbow disappears ultimately leaving behind only a limitless sky, similarly the worshipper of the Saguṇa ultimately comes to the stage of realizing that the object of his worship is the Infinite, the Absolute.[18]

The Bhāgavata has thus tried to achieve a transformation of human tendencies through the soft, pleasant, and perfumed path of devotion. And let us not forget that it has been very much successful in its object. It has wielded more influence than the Upanishads, has saved more lives from being lost, than any other scripture, has inspired many lives for dedicating their heart and soul to the upliftment of society[19], and has given new tone of sublimation to literature.[20]

Emphasis on Bhakti :

We find, therefore, that the Bhāgavata has given immense importance to bhakti.

The Bhagavata, as per the statement of Brahmā, is teaching of the Supreme Himself. Its object being the generating of bhakti, it contains an account of the superhuman powers (vibhūtis) of God.[21]

And the Bhagavata has really tried time and again to persuade readers to cultivate a sense of sincere devotion towards God. "The biggest duty of man is to cultivate bhakti for God—a bhakti which is selfless and devoid of any obstruction," declares the Bhāgavata.[22] Even if a man does all his duties but lacks a devotion for the Supreme, his entire labour is just useless.[23] God should be made an object of recitation, remembrance, and meditation.[24]

When Parīkṣita asks Śukadeva, "who is the object of hearing, meditating, and remembering for all the beings of the world, "Śukadeva tells him: "Any person who wants a position unaffected by any kind of fear whatsoever should hear Hari, recite Hari's name, and love Him."[25]

In the world there is no path more auspicious and beneficial than the path of Devotion in Vāsudeva.[26]

Brahma who minutely studied the Vedas thrice came to the conclusion that there is no other way more auspicious and propitious than the path of bhakti.[27]

The gain of human life, knowledge, and discharging of duties is a constant memory of Nārāyaṇa.[28] Devahūti is told that the supreme well-being of human life comes through an intense devotion to God with a stable and firm dedication of mind to the Supreme.[29]

Only that action is action which satisfies God, and only that learning is real learning that helps in concentrating our mind on God.[30]

God is the inner being of all the embodied selves, He is the Lord of Nature. Therfore if human beings seek the shelter at His feet, that would be very propitious for them.[31]

Man should not forget that only that birth is real birth, only that activity is real activity whereby Lord Hari is served.[32]

Just as when we water the roots of a tree, water reaches every leaf and branch of a tree; in the same way, if we propitiate God, all the gods become pleased.[33]

Yamarāja clearly states in the Bhāgavata in the story of Ajāmila that the supreme duty of human beings in this world is to seek bhakti of the lord through a recital of His names, glories meditation etc.[34]

Prahlāda advises his friends to cultivate a concentrated and exclusive bhakti for the Supreme and see Him everywhere.[35] The Bhāgavata is of the firm opinion that the Supreme who is beyond being and non-being, and though attributeless, appears to be full of attributes, can be realized only through a devout devotion.[36]

Though God is not realizable easily through dravya, deśa, kāla and other sacrificial instruments, yet He is very kind to the devottees.[37]

He is Infinite and is surely devoid of any natural name or form. But whosoever serves His feet enjoys the privilege of His play-sports wherein He assumes many names and forms to please His devotees. Though He resides in the hearts of all, yet He assumes different forms in accordance with the feelings of the devotees just as though air is essentially devoid of smell etc. but assumes smell of the scent. Thus the feelings of the individuals are the scents in accordance with which the Supreme assumes different forms.[38]

The Supreme is like the Kalpa-taru (the tree that has the power of granting anything desired under it). One gets the gain in due accordance with one's devotion, for there is nothing like big or small for the Lord. All are just equal.[39]

The Bhāgavata has described the Supreme many times by the terms that show that he likes the path of devotion as a way of attaining the Ultimate Truth beyond any doubt. For example, the Supreme has been described as auspicious for the world[40], giver of boons to the distressed and poor[41], exceedingly auspicious, giver of welfare, very kind, the support of the world[42], bliss by nature, one realizable through experience alone[43], the creator of all religions[44], excessively kind hearted,[45] the Father, the Preceptor and the Master of the world,[46] most intimately friendly to all,[47] attractor of the god of love[48], the refuge of the noble[49], the lover of the lowly[50], giver of all the desires like the Kalpa tree,[51] magnificence, strength, knowledge, beauty, renown etc.[52], one who does not know any difference,[53] the beauty of the world,[54] one who is free from every blemish[55] etc.

Why these adjectives have been used for the Supreme by the Bhāgavata ? The answer is very clear. These adjectives have been used to impress upon the minds of the common people the desirability of cultivating a sincere and firm devotion for the Supreme conceived in the form of Kṛṣṇa.[56]

After all the sole object of knowledge is to realize the truth by the process of eradication of the sensual and the material. Unless mind is free from the attachments for the mundane materials, one cannot hope to get the Truth.

But since the path of knowledge is strewn with many a pitfall and lacks the prospects of being liked by the common man, some other way has to be found out. As Sūta states in the Bhāgavata Māhātmya, the basic question of human life is to free the Self from the clutches of death. The Bhāgavata way of devotion is that way which charms a human heart and, at the same time, frees him from the danger of death.[57]

The very circumstances in which the Bhāgavata is reported to have been narrated to Parīkṣit establishes this fact. He had a very limited period to live. He knew that he would die by a particular time. The basic question before Śukadeva was how to dispel the fear of death from his mind. To state the same thing in a philosophical language, the basic problem before Śukadeva was to liberate Parīkṣit mentally. This feat was to be accomplished within a very short duration.

It was possible for Śukadeva to say that the life is small but one does not die by the so-called deaths. Real death to this world of suffering comes only when the truth is realized that an individual is not just an individual. He is the infinite, immortal, ageless, deathless Supreme Reality Himself. But to repeat these things verbally would not make a person free from the dangers of death and life, sufferings and agonies. It takes a long time, even many lives to realize this Truth. Parīkṣit who was a king and must have done many things that would give him a sense of guilt at that crucial hour of his life, was obviously not in position to undertake this arduous journey of the world of knowledge. He thought that he was doomed. The pressing problem before Śuka was, therefore, to free his heart from these sentiments which made him more and more nervous.

Therefore by teaching Parīkṣit the way of devotion in the form of the Bhāgavata, Śuka made an attempt to convince the doomed king that if he dedicates himself wholly to the Lord nothing but good would come to him. The Lord is very kind hearted and helpful. Even the most wretched man can get liberation, if he seeks the bhakti of the Lord sincerely.[58] When one comes under the protecting care of the Supreme, it is but natural that his fear should disappear. Faith in the Almighty gives a trembling heart courage and conviction and the subsequent satisfaction.[59]

Not only does a trembling heart gets courage and strength, he gets the supreme knowledge. In the language of the Bhāgavata, any one who serves God, cultivates a love for Him, gets an experience of his real nature, and develops a sense of renunciation for the earthly objects is like a man who takes meals and thereby gets satisfaction, strength, and dispelling of hunger simultaneously.[60] As a matter of fact knowledge and renunciation are the sons of bhakti.[61]

Lest it should be thought that the path of devotion is inferior to the path of knowledge, it has been made clear that the matter is not like that. A devotee is in no way inferior. On the other hand the Supreme cannot be realized so easily by any penance, or recital of the Vedas, or cultivation of knowledge as by the devotion.[62] The example of the cowherd women is before us to give us conviction in the matter.

The Bhāgavata has been written to produce elements of bhakti, jñāna, and virāga, devotion, knowledge, and renunciation in the human heart.[63]

As a matter of religious and spiritual fact, every individual is a 'parīkṣit' because just as King Parīkṣit was called 'parīkṣit' because he was examining all the people coming in his contact to find out who, out of them all, was the person whom Parīkṣit saw in his mother's womb, similarly every individual tries to find out the Supreme with whom he was intimately connected when he began his departure to this land of mortality. Just as King Parīkṣit was cursed by Sṛñgī to be bitten by the serpent Takṣaka, every individual self is accursed to be bitten by death.[64]

Considered from this point of view, every individual self is facing the extinction of his life. The fear of death is gnawing at his feet. Like Parīkṣit, every individual self is short of time due to his preoccupation with worldly life, generally speaking.

Therefore, the path of devotion, as delineated by the Bhāgavata is the best way of seeking liberation from the fears and horrors of worldly life. It is the way that can untie the knot of a man's heart, can destroy all his doubts, and enfeeble his mundane activities.[65] It is possible to get liberation by pursuing the path of bhakti with sincerity and integrity.[66]

Bhakti defined

Bhakti implies an intimate and intense love for God. A devotee fixes his attention on the feet of God alone and spurns anything that comes by way of an obstruction in the path of this love.[67] God is thought to be beloved, father, mother, brother everything. Bhakti consists in dedicating all the actions performed through body, language, mind, intelligence etc to God with sincerity and honesty.[68]

An instance of such dedication of actions is provided by the Gopīs. They used to recite the name of Śrī Kṛṣṇa with a heart full of love, and eyes full of tears while taking out milk from the breasts of cows, threshing rice, churning curds, cleaning the house, and doing everything else of the kind.[69] What is needed is a self-less service of God.[70] What is essential is a selfless service of the godhead.[71] In a real devotion there is simply a desire for God. Even a desire for obtaining the position of Bramhā, the creator, or the abode of India, or the empire of the world, or even liberation is absent there.[72] What is really needed is a mind deeply and firmly attached to God.[73] God demands a complete, willing surrender on the part of a devotee.[74]

The Bhāgavata is of this opinion that bhakti implies a willing selfless surrender to God. It means a firm, stable, and unflinching attachment for God, which is unaffected by any personal desire, or worldly ambition. Bhakti is thus a transforming experience. It is a transforming experience because a God-oriented attitude is produced in a devotee that brings about a complete change in the attitude of the latter towards the world. His tendencies, which were formerly directed towards worldly desires and aspiration, mundane ambitions, or attainment of superhuman powers, or even liberation from the world, are suddenly turned completely towards God. A devotee no doubt, lives a worldly life. But he does not live for himself. He lives only for his God, his beloved. He becomes a shadow of his master. His heart is full of love for his beloved, his mind is full of admiration for his beloved, his body moves for his beloved. A life of devotion is a life that is no longer personal. It belongs to God alone. The reason is obvious. The mental tendencies of a devotee are surrendered at the feet of God, his speech invariably engaged in reciting His names, and his body is always in the state of paying an obeisance to Him.[75]

A devotee wishes to fix his mind on God alone in every life and in every condition.[76] Because a mind that is devoted to God plays in the ocean of nectar. He is not interested in the dirty water of a ditch of worldly pleasure or heavenly attractions.[77]

If we want to have in one word the definition of bhakti, we can get it in the Bhāgavata in the words of Prahlāda, the paragon of devotees. According to him devotion consists in dedicating mind, speech, actions, riches and life to God.[78] Yes, devotion is a state of perpetual dedication to God. This dedication is so complete that ego is completely obliterated and only the Lord remains. The devotee becomes the Lord Himself because the lines that divide and go to make an individual fall down, and a sense of intimate, hearty unity emerges between the devotee and the object of devotion.[79] Unless the individual self is transcended and transmuted into the object of devotion, the state of devotion is not reached. The definition of bhakti as given by the Śāṅdilya Sūtra, therefore, comes very near the definition of bhakti emanating from the Bhāgavata. The Śāṅdilya Sūtra has defined bhakti as an intense love for God.[80] According to the Bhāgavata, as we have seen, bhakti is a state of complete dedication of life, mind, and everything else, out of the supreme attachment developed for God. The Bhāgavata has tried to illustrate this point by depicting the lives of Prahlāda, and the Gopīs with gusto and brilliance.

Prahlāda was so attached to God that he did not care for his father, material prosperity, prestige, and even his life's security. The Gopīs were similarly so attached to God that they did not care for their relatives or the opinions of their caste and community.

We, therefore, can safely conclude that according to the Bhāgavata, a sense of supreme dedication and utmost attachment to God, the Beloved, is the mark of devotion.

And since there is a worldly consideration present in devotion, the factors of caste, sex, family, pedigree etc. are quite immaterial for bhakti.[81]

The Characteristic features of a devotee

The Bhāgavata has tried to present a list of those traits which can be termed to be the characteristic features of a devotee.[82] These marks of a devotee also help us in arriving at the essence of bhakti.

According to the Bhāgavata a devotee is kindhearted. He is kind to one and all. His heart is devoid of any sense of animosity towards anybody. He is forbearing and patient. He is truthful to the core of his heart, and is free from every blemish. He is equal to all and quite impartial. He always tries to do good to others. His mind is free from all worldly desires. By nature he is self-restrained, lovable and affable, and a person of morally perfect conduct. He is destitute and selfless. He does not eat much and loves peace. He is unperturbed, and invariably seeks the shelter of the feet of the Lord. He is given to meditation. He does not make mistakes and is sober by temperament. He never loses fortitute and courage. He is the controller of six guṇas viz. hunger, thirst, sorrow, attachment, birth and death. He never seeks any honour for himself, but always tries to give respect to others. He is very expert in making others understand the truth about God, and is friendly to all. He is full of pity and sympathy for others, and is the knower of Truth. He does not care for the Vedic injunctions and rites and rituals and is the servant of God, leaving all other religious conventions.

This list of the traits of a devotee also suggests to us that a man of devotion is solely attached to God, and mentally detached to worldly pleasures and aspirations. He leads a life that is detached to the worldly objects, free from any tinge of selfishness, and attached to the Lord.[83]

Types of Bhakti

The Bhāgavata mentions different types of bhakti at different places. It would be interesting to study these types of bhakti here and try to find out the truth emerging from this study.

(1) Three Kinds of bhakti

We find that at two places three types of bhakti have been suggested in the Bhāgavata. These three kinds of bhakti are respectively, hearing about God, reciting the glories and names of God, and remembering God.[84]

2) *Four Kinds of bhakti*

At another occasion we come across a mention of four types of devotion. Hearing about God, reciting His glories and names, meditating upon Him, and Worshipping Him, are the four types of bhakti.[85]

(3) Five Kinds of bhakti

Śrutadeva has made a mention of five kinds of bhakti viz. recital of God's glories by speech, hearing the stories of God, doing service of God with hands, remembering God and His deeds, and fixing mind on the feet of the Supreme Lord. The five types of bhakti are hearing about God's glory, reciting His glories, worshipping images, respecting God, and discussing with others about God.[86]

(4) Six Kinds of bhakti

Nala and Kubara who were liberated by Śrī Kṛṣṇa have mentioned six kinds of bhakti. They are reciting the glory of God by speech, hearing God's stories with ears, serving the Lord with hands, fixing mind on the feet of the Lord, remembering Him and His glories, and paying obeisance to the world which is the abode of the Lord.[87]

(5) Seven Kinds of bhakri

Here the term bhakti has to be interpreted rather liberally. If we understand the term liberally, Kapila suggests seven kinds of devotion to attain the Lord, viz. performing our social duties in a selfless manner, an intense attachment for the Lord, knowledge yielding the Truth, strong sense of renunciation, penances, hearing of the scriptures, and performing meditation or samādhi.[88]

(6) Nine Kinds of bhakti

The most popular and famous kinds of bhakti are nine. These kinds are mentioned by Prahlāda to his father Hiraṇyakaśipu. These kinds of bhakti are reciting God's name, hearing God's glories, remembering Him, serving His feet, worshipping Him, paying obeisance to Him, cultivating a sense of friendship with Him, and surrendering oneself at the feet of the Lord.[89]

(7) Ten Kinds of bhakti

In a way Śaunaka suggests ten kinds of bhakti. Hearing the glory of the Lord, reciting the glory of the Lord, paying respect to the Lord, serving the Lord with hands, seeing the statue reminding the Lord, or river and the sacred places reminding one about the Lord, visiting the places where the Lord had done His līlās or sport-like acts, seeking the company of the saints and paying them respect, enjoying the perfume of Tulasī leaf kept at the feet of the Lord, cultivating a heart that would feel the warmth of emotion at the very name of the Lord, and feeling joy at the hearing of saints' speech.[90]

(8) *Eleven Kinds of bhakti*

King Aṁbrīśa practised eleven kinds of devotion.

He always remembered the feet of Śrī Kṛṣṇa. His speech always found joy in reciting the glories and līlās of Śrī Kṛṣṇa. He used to serve God with his hands as he woulds cleanse the temple of the Lord with his own hands. His ears were always engaged in the hearing of the līlās of Kṛṣṇa. His nose would enjoy the smell of the leaf of Tulsī tree kept at the feet of the Lord, his tongue used to enjoy the Naivedya offered to the Lord. His feet were usually busy touring the region where the Lord performed His līlās. And finally he surrendered the objects of enjoyment like garland, sandal etc to the Lord.[90a]

(9) *Twelve kinds of bhakti*

Nārada narrated twelve kinds of bhakti to Prahlāda.

It has been mentioned that these are the ways of cultivating self-less love for the Lord.[91]

The kinds of bhakti enumerated here are service of the teacher, dedicating whatever one possesses to the Lord, seeking the good company of the saints and devotees, worship of the Lord, keeping faith in the stories of God, reciting His glories and name, meditation of His feet, seeing and worshipping His temples and images, fulfilling desires of others with tbis idea that the Lord resides everywhere, respecting others heartily, and conquering the six guṇas viz. kama, anger, avarice, attachment, malice etc.[92]

(10) *Thirteen kinds of bhakti*

On one occasion Srī Kṛṣṇa narrated thirteen kinds of bhakti to Uddhava, viz. performing all the actions for the Lord, remembering the Lord while performing any act, dedicating mind and heart to the Lord, residing at the places where the devotees reside, imitating the persons devoted to the Lord, celebrating the festivals etc. with music, dances etc., seeing the Lord in oneself and all others, respecting all people, keeping even attitude towards the Brahmin, Cāṅādala, thief and a person respecting Brahmin, the sun and a spark, the kind-hearted and the cruel, dispelling rivalry envy, disrespect, pride from the heart, not caring for the ridicule of others, destroying the sense of shame due to public opinion or bodily condition, paying respect to even a cow and a donkey by laying prostrate on ground.[93]

(*11*) *Fifteen kinds of bhakti*

On another occasion Śrīkṛṣṇa narrates a scheme of fifteen kinds of bhakti to Uddhava. These kinds are, cultivating faith in the sweet stories of the Lord, constant recital of His glories, firm faith in worshipping, addressing panegyrics to the Lord, respecting the devotees, loving the service of God, lying prostrate before God, seeing God in every being, performing every activity for Him, reciting his glories with speech, dedicating the very mind to Him, leaving every other desire excepting a desire for God, sacrificing riches, objects of enjoyment and material comforts, performing sacrifices, giving alms, observing fasts etc. for Him alone.[94]

(*12*) *Eighteen kinds of bhakti*

Kapila unfolds a plan of eighteen kinds of bhakti before his mother Devahūti consisting of practising the path of yoga like restraint, etc. with faith, developing full faith in the Lord, hearing His stories, considering all the beings equal, maintaining friendliness with all, celibacy, observing silence, performing the social and religious actions honestly, satisfaction at whatever is provided by providence, taking meals in a small quantity, cultivating a tendency of meditation, remaining lonely, peacefulness of nature, brother to all, having pity and sympathy for all, courageous temperament, free from a sense of ego due to the knowledge of Prakṛti and Puruṣa, seeing nothing but the Lord everywhere etc.[95]

(*13*) *Nineteen kinds of bhakti*

Sanatkumāra has given a scheme of nineteen kinds of bhakti. They are keeping faith in the words of a teacher and scriptures, practising the duties of the devotees, curiosity for the ultimate knowledge, stable faith in the path of knowledge, worship of Śrīkṛṣṇa, listening to the stories of the Lord, abstaining from the parties of the people immersed in sensual pleasure, not storing the things they like, living in solitude, not injuring anybody, faith in renunciation, seeking the welfare of the real self, enjoying the flavour of the glories of the Lord, etc.[96]

(14) Twenty kinds of bhakti

On another occasion Kapila narrates twenty kinds of bhakti to his mother Devahūti viz. performance of one's duties, performing nonviolent rites, having 'darśana' of God's idols, touching them, worshipping them, addressing panegyrics to them, paying respect to them, considering all beings as the abodes of the Lord, fortitude, renunciation, respect of the great souls, pity for the poor, friendship towards the people of equal status, following the rules of restraint etc., listening to the spiritual scriptures, reciting the names of the Lord loudly, straightforwardness of mind, seeking company of the good people, renunciation of the pride etc.[97]

(15) Twenty-four kinds of bhakti

Śrī Kṛṣṇa tells Uddhava about some twenty-four types of bhakti on one occasion. They consist of the darśana of the devotees and the images of the Lord, touching them, worshipping them, rendering service to them, addressing panegyrics to them, recital of Lord's names and glories, faith in the listening to the Lord's stories, constant meditation of the Lord, dedicating everything to the Lord, surrendering everything to the Lord, the master, talking about the noble births and deeds of the Lord, celebrating the festivals like Kṛṣṇa Janma etc. learning the Vedic and the Tāntric ways of worship, journeying the places of the Lord's activities, installing idols in the temples, building temples, gardens, play fields etc. for the Lord, cleansing the temples in the spirit of the servent of the Lord, never taking pride in this service in the spirit of superiority, dedicating everything to the Lord, placing the dearest thing at the feet of the Lord etc.[98]

(16) Twenty-five kinds of bhakti

Kapila narrates twenty-five kinds of bhakti to his mother Devahūti such as performing one's duties, following the injunctions of the Vedas, satisfaction at the receipt of anything obtained due to providence, worshipping the men of knowledge, abstaining from the acts that contribute to an increase of sensual nature, loving religions that free a man from the bondage of the world, taking pious and limited food, residing in a solitary place, not harming any being by body, mind, or speech, speaking the truth, avoiding stealing, not to amass more than the things absolutely essential, abstaining from sexual union, performing a penance, keeping clean internally and externally, studying scriptures, worshipping the Lord, keeping restraint over speech, meditating on the Self, practising good postures (āsanas), etc.[99]

(17) Twenty-six types of bhakti

Ṛṣabhadeva preached twenty-six types of bhakti to his sons. They are respecting the teacher, renouncing avarice, bearing the pleasures and the pain serenely, thinking that a self has to face difficulties etc. in every birth, seeking the Ultimate Truth, undertaking penances, renouncing an action prompted by a desire, performing action only for the Lord, listening to the Lord's stories, seeking the company of the people of devotion, reciting the Lord's glories abstaining from animosity, equanimity, peacefulness, love for solitude, abstaining from egoistic feeling, study of spiritual scriptures, complete self-restraint, etc.[100]

(18) Thirty kinds of bhakti

Nārada pointed out thirty charactristics of dharma which can be equated with devotion, such as truthfulness, kindness, penance performance, cleanliness, forbearance, discrimination, mental restraint, nonviolence, celibacy, sacrifice, study of the scriptures, straightforwardness, self-contentedness, service of the even minded saints, gradual renunciation from the mundane enjoyments, want of pride, love for silence, self-meditation, equal division of corn, seeing the Lord in all persons, listening to the Lord's glories, their recital, their remembrance, His service, respect for Him, a sense of servitude for the Lord, sense of friendliness with the Lord, a sense of self-surrender.[101]

(19) Thirty-six types of bhakti

The seer Prabuddha tells about thirty-six types of bhakti to Videha. He also talks about a sense of detachment, good company of the devotees, kindness, respect for all, penance, forbearance, study of the scriptures, self-restraint etc. [102] Thus we find that the Bhāgavata gives us many types of bhakti. It is clear that these classifications of bhakti cannot be exhaustive. There can be as many ways of worshipping God as there are individuals inhabiting the earth.

We come across, however, in the Bhāgavata a very important and thoughtful classification of bhakti. According to this classification, bhakti can be divided in two kinds viz. saguṇa bhakti and the nirguṇa bhakti.

The Saguṇa bhakti is a devotion marked by certain desire on the part of the devotee. This desire has some tinge of selfish motive behind it. And as there can be three kinds of desires—the mundane ones, we find three types of the Saguṇa bhakti. The first and the lowest bhakti is Tāmasa bhakti wherein a devotee worships the Lord with a desire of undertaking a revenging approach. He wants to harm his enemy. Or he is envious of the prosperity of some person. Or he wants to demonstrate his superiority over the rest of the people.

The second type of bhakti is the Rājasa bhakti. It is superior to the Tāmasa bhakti. In Rājasa bhakti, a devotee worships the Lord in some particular form and worships Him for getting riches or renown.

The third type of Saguṇa bhakti is the Sātvika bhakti. It is the best bhakti in this category. In this bhakti a devotee worships the Lord for destroying his sins, or seeking His affection or love.

But even this Sātvika Saguṇa bhakti does not go very far. It cannot be the ideal of divine love, for it contains traces of some desire even in its highest flight. When one transcends the region of the Saguṇa bhakti, one comes to the land of the Nirguṇa bhakti.

The Nirguṇa bhakti is marked by a desireless state of mind and is devoid of any distinction or difference. A selfless, wholly dedicated spirit is present in the Nirguṇa bhakti. A person who has cultivated the Nirguṇa bhakti does not care even for the various places like the Sālokya (residence in the eternal abode of the Lord), Sārṣṭi (enjoying the pleasure like God), Sāmīpya (the eternal proximity of the Lord), Sārūpya (gaining the form like that of the Lord), and Sāyujya (identification with the Supreme).[103]

The Nirguṇa bhakti is the highest development of bhakti. It is the ideal that an enlightened devotee keeps in his mind and ever aspires to reach.

In a way the Nirguṇa bhakti reminds us about the highest objective found in region of knowledge. Just as a person who has attained the state of Brahmanhood, or realized the ideal of "So aham" (I am That) cannot be swerved from that highest stage and is completely dead to the worldly desires of every kind and description, in the similar manner a person who has realized the ideal of the Nirguṇa bhakti is devoid of anything mundane in character. Just as a person who has attained the highest stage of knowledge becomes the absolute himself, in the same manner the person who has cultivated the Nirguṇa bhakti becomes the Supreme himself to all intents and purposes, for he sees his Lord everywhere including in his own heart and mind. Like the Gopīs, he becomes the very images of God.[104]

This type of interpretation of the Nirguṇa bhakti is not unjustified if we remember that according to the Bhāgavata the knowledge and renunciation are the sons of bhakti.[105] In the Bhāgavata the path of bhakti is in no way antagonistic to the path of jñāna.[106] Even Prahlāda, the supreme devotee, has made it clear that the Lord is perfect. He does not need the worship of the unlearned. He, however, accepts the worship from the people out of compassion. The benefit of this worship too goes to the people themselves. Just as the beauty of the face beautifies even the reflection reflected in the mirror, in the same way whatever respect is paid to the Lord by a devotee, is a respect by the later to himself.[107]

The Bhāgavata from the very beginning is aware of the ultimate nature of the Supreme Truth.[108] And there is no basic difference between the Lord and the devotee from the point of view of the metaphysical truth.[109] The devotee must know that ultimately he worships the Formless Infinite.[110]

The Bhāgavata condemns any attitude that differentiates between the Lord and the devotee in the ultimate stage.[111] The worship of an idol is just a means of getting the ultimate stage.[112] The ultimate truth is that there is only but one Truth.[113] Only the persons of immature intelligence see the Lord only in the idols.[114]

Worship of the idols

Since the Bhāgavata believes in a gradual rise of an individual in the realm of thought, it does not decry even the idol worship. On the other hand it gives it the respect it deserves.[115] In fact in the twenty-seventh chapter of the Skandha eleven, the Bhāgavata proceeds to deal with the question of idol worship with enough details. It gives the description of eight kinds of statues and idols viz. those made of stone, wood, metal, earth, sandal wood, sand etc.[116] It mentions threc methods of worship of idols viz, the Vedic, Tāntrika, and the Mixed.[117]

But the Bhāgavata makes it clear that what is important in this idol worship is sincerity and faith.[118] The Lord is pleased even with water offered with faith.[119] What is desirable is to worship the Lord with a mind free from worldly desires. Thereby the person is initiated in the path of devotion.[120]

Uddhava asks a question about the easiest way of obtaining the highest position in the realm of god-realization. And Śrī Kṛṣṇa points out that devotion is the easiest method of realizing the Supreme. When a person attains a state of complete dedication, he becomes immortal.[121] When one drinks this nectar of devotion, there remains nothing for him to know.[122]

The Saguṇa and the Nirguṇa

Sometimes a question is asked, how a devotion to the Saguṇa can be compatible with the knowledge of the Nirguṇa?

In answer to this query, I would like to quote the words of Vinoba Bhāve.

"Though the stream of bhakti springs from saguna, it reaches nirguna in the end." Writes Vinoba Bhave. "Here is an old story. I had gone to Vaikom to observe the satyagraha there. I remembered the geographical fact that Sankaracharya birthplace was on the border of Malabar. I had a feeling that Sankara's village, Kaladi, was somewhere near. I asked the Malayali genlteman who accompanied me. He said, "It is some 10 or 12 miles from here. Do you want to go there ? I said I did not. I was going to see the satyagraha in progress, and it did not seem proper to go elsewhere. So on that occasion I did not go to that village. Even now it seems to me that I was right in not going there then. But that night when I went to bed, that village of Kaladi and the image of Sankaracharya stood before my eyes again and again. I could not sleep. That experience is still with me, as fresh today as it was then. Again and again that night, I thought of Sankaracharya the power of his jnana, his divine certitude in advaita, the extraordinary, glowing vairagya, non-attachment, which convinced him that samsara, this phenomenal life, was all false, of the majesty of his language and the boundless help I have received from him. All night long these images stood before me. Then I realized how nirguna is filled to the brim with saguna. Even seeing him face to face would not have evoked such love. Even nirguna is filled with saguna. For the most part, I do not write letters to friends to enquire about their welfare. But even when I do not write to a friend, the thought of him is ever present, it fills my mind. Thus, saguna lies hidden in nirguna. Saguna and nirguna are indeed one. Placing an image before us and worshipping it with visible outward service, on the one hand, and on the other hand, being constantly concerned inwardly with the world's welfare, while performing no outward acts of worship—both these have the same worth and value."[123]

Yes, Vinoba is right. Whatever is in our mind tries to express itself in some form or the other. Even if we worship the Absolute, our mind has a tendency of giving it some form, some shape. One may call it *Aum*, others may call it Kṛṣṇa, or Rāma or Śiva or some other name may be given to this Supreme Reality.

If this is the psychology of human mind, the Saguṇa cannot be either ignored or condemned. A person who is starting his journey in the domain of the knowledge of the Supreme, must begin in the way acceptable to his nature. Just as the corn is hidden in the husk, and the coconut is hidden in its hard cover, the Supreme is hidden in the Saguṇa, the Nirguṇa is lurking in the embodied God.

Śrī Kṛṣṇa who is the Supreme is not just a son of Vāsudeva and Devakī. The Bhāgavata sees in Him the Brahman.[124] Even the love-lorn Gopīs know this truth.[125] The various panegyrics addressed to Śrī Kṛṣṇa viz Akrūra Stuti[126] Brahmā Stuti[127] and many others have been introduced by the Bhāgavata to show the fact that according to the Bhāgavata, Śrī-Kṛṣṇa is the Absolute.[128]

The sage Pippalāyana gives the quintessence of the Bhāgavata view of Śrī Kṛṣṇa when he states :

"O King, know the Ultimate Reality to be Nārāyaṇa who is responsible for the creation, maintenance and destruction of this universe, though Himself attributable to no cause; who persists, within as well as without, in all the three stages of dream, waking life, and sound sleep and who inspires and stirs the body along with its various sense organs, the respiratory system and the heart to their respective functions. Just as sparks cannot penetrate the fire, in the same way our mind, speech, eyes, intellect, respiratory organs and sense organs are incapable of comprehending that Ultimate Principle ; nay, they cannot even approach it. He was never born and shall never die; He does not grow, nor does He ever diminish in size; He is immune from changes like birth and death, but is only a witness of all changing conditions; He is present everywhere and at every time and shall ever remain so; He is imperishable and consists of knowledge and knowledge alone. Just as vitality is one, although it functions differently through the different organs (for instance, the eyes see, the ears hear, nose smells, and so on and so forth), and thus appears as differentiated, in the same way, the Ātman though one, appears as differentiated, because of its manifesting itself through bodies. God is present every where—in the whole creation—alike in mammals such as the human being, the cow, the horse, the elephant, the lion, the dog, the sheep, the goat etc; in birds and other hatched creatures; in insects-bred by sweat and the refuse of the body etc. and the vegetable world which springs up from the soil; in short, wherever there is vitality functioning in some form or other. That which is seen abiding in us as a constant witnessing factor even when all our senses are dormant, nay, even when the 'ego' is expressed by the words 'I am' lapses for a time, and which we call to our mind, on our waking, by using such expressions as "We had a good sleep", "We saw this dream", and so on, is Brahman."[129]

The Bhāgavata reaches to the highest flight of metaphysical insight when it states : "At the beginning of creation I alone subsisted, the One beyond the manifest and the unmanifest, and nothing else. And it is I alone who survive the creation. This phenomenal world is nothing but myself, and whatever remains after that is also myself."[130]

This idea is comparable with the central idea of the famous Nāsadīya Sūkta which states : "The darkness prevailed everywhere before the creation of this universe. In the midst of that darkness and even beyond, He subsisted, all by Himself, One Glorious Being, consisting of nothing but intelligence and having no origin other than Himself He evolved Himself out of the darkness and created the universe "[131]

Similarly, it can be compared with the following observation of the Upanishads: "The Brahman is perfect and pervading in every way. This creation is also filled with Him, as this perfect universe is born from Him alone. In this way, the universe is replete with the perfection of the Brahman. Even if we subduct this perfect universe from the Perfect Brahman we get only the Perfect as reminder."[132]

The Saguṇa is thus not a fiction even according to the above quoted statement. The whole world is but an embodiment of the Supreme. The Ṛgveda mentions it.[133] The Bhagavadgītā states this.[134] The Māṇḍūkya Upanishad writes this [135] The Śvetāśvatara mentions it [136] And the Bhāgavata too points out to this fact [137]

The Bhāgavata tries to lead a worshipper from the idol to the universe as the image of the Supreme. In fact it tries to lead a person following the path of knowledge and devotion to the highest possible realization of the metaphysical truth.[138] But if one does not want to forget the ultimate nature of the Supreme Truth, one has to remember that in the ultimate analysis the Truth must be formless and abstract. Every form, howsoever vast and comprehensive it may be, suffers from some limitations.

It is possible that a person may consider only the saguṇa as the sole reality. And then, if sufficient care is not taken to make advance in the desirable direction, the saguṇa may lead to factions and sects. And that may lead to a fight waged in the name of God. As Swāmi Vivekananda put it : "All the different ideas of God, which are more or less materialistic, must go. As man becomes more and more spiritual he has to throw off all these ideas and leave them behind."[139]

Vinoba Bhave also expresses similar opinion.

"Saguna is not only easy but free from danger, but it needs nirguna to complete it," writes Vinoba Bhave. "As saguna grows the flower of nirguna, of devotion to principle, should blossom. Nirguna and saguna complement each other, they are not incompatible. Starting from saguna, one has to tread the path to the goal of nirguna; nirguna, too, needs the waters of saguna to cleanse the subtle impurities of the mind. Each gains lusture from the other."[140]

The Bhāgavata, therefore, shares this view that though the Supreme is Formless and Knowledge, He becomes embodied, saguṇa, for the sake of the devotees.[141]

The Bhāgavata clearly states that the Supreme is all, both saguṇa and the nirguṇa.[142] But its faith is in the Nirguṇa.[143] The very first śloka of the Bhāgavata leaves no doubt as to the fact that the Bhāgavata pins its faith on the Absolute.[144] Even in the concluding chapter the Bhāgavata writes about the Absolute alone.[145] It is even stated that the Bhāgavata is the essence of all Vedāntic thought.[146] Lest there should be any doubt, it is stated that the subject-matter of the Bhāgavata is pure knowledge.[147] And the sole object of the Bhāgavata is the Supreme Truth.[148]

A question that can be asked is how this Absolute can become Śrī Kṛṣṇa ? The answer to the question lies in the concept of Līlā. There are several passages in the Bhāgavata that indicate that the Supreme became Śrī Kṛṣṇa through Līlā.[149] The concept of Līlā is as old as the Upanishads. The Bṛahadāraṇyaka says, "Everybody sees His sport (this creation), but Himself no one sees."[150]

In the similar vein the Bhāgavata has only one answer to the question of the creation of the world, the appearance of many when the reality is single, non-dual principle. "He creates, maintains and destroys this world by Līlā without being attached enjoys all the objects lurking in the Jīvas nonattachedly by Lila," writes the Bhāgavata's author.[151] "He accepts Prakṛti to do playful acts whereby this creation goes on."[152] God is playing making Himself a toy.[153] He assumes many Forms to play on this earth.[154]

Now the term Lilā means sport which is the free expression of the internal dynamic consciousness of joy, beauty and fullness of the player.

But this Līlā is not a mere play as ordinarily understood. Līlā is not to be taken in the sense of a pastime or play or sport, as there cannot possibly be any motive or necessity for Him to resort to them. It only suggests that He has no special purpose and that He is not constrained by any external agency or desire. His activities are only a spontaneous overflow of the fullness of His own bliss like the activities of a man of realization. It also suggests the effortlessness, ease, and pleasure with which He undertakes activities, and complete independence of others for help."[155]

In the Chapter seven, skandha three, of the Bhāgavata, Vidura expresses a doubt before Maitreya as to how the Great Lord should think of a sport ? He is devoid of any desires and wants and completely free from attachments, why should any thought of sport enter His mind ?[156]

The reply that is given is, that it is all Māyā.

We should construe the term Līla as such in the sense of a "mysterious act" or sham act."[157] The sense of sport no doubt goes to some extent to show the nature of God's act. But obviously it does not go very far. The Bhāgavata has probably used the term līla to distinguish human act, sport included, from the act of the Supreme in a typical sense.

Construed in this way, Līlā throws utmost light on the acts of God. No better word can be found for the purpose. The term līlā implies a seeming reality of the creation and at the same time emphasizes the ultimate unsubstantiality of this universe. This would be clear from one example.

Suppose there is an actor. Now the actor has to play many roles. At times he may die in the drama. But actually he is unaffected by this death or the various changed garbs assumed by him. But the play, while it is taken by the spectator as a pleasant play which absorbs him in that process, is a reality. The Supreme in the similar manner plays certain roles by creating, maintaining and destroying this universe or taking up the bodies of Rāma, Śrī Kṛṣṇa etc. The wise person can understand that this body or act is only superficial. The artificial garb of the Supreme cannot mislead a wise spectator of this drama of creation.

And yet this drama has a purpose. The Supreme tries to show to the people that they are not just individuals, suffering and dying. They have to be taught the Supreme Truth that they are the sparks of the same fire.[158] The various Līlās of the Supreme are just attempts to help the persons realize that they are not miserable creatures.

Attracted by the beauty, might, strength, majesty etc. of the Supreme, the individuals worship them in the form of Śrīkṛṣṇa, Rāma, Śiva, Ganeśa or any other deity, but are ultimately led to the position that the Supreme's ultimate form lies much beyond.[159]

It has been clearly indicated that whosoever recites the līlās of the Lord gets the devotion of the Supreme who is the objective of the great liberated souls.[160] There has been an attempt to emphasize the fact that the Bhāgavata is an attempt aimed at the exposition of the Brahman.[161]

A question may be asked : how recital of names and exploits of the Lord can lead to the ultimate stage? The answer to this question is very simple. It is a psychological fact that if we recite anything daily with interest and faith, we get attached to it. Attachment to the Supreme in this way is developed. And this attachment to the Lord means the detachment from the mundane objects and freedom of human heart and mind from the dirt of selfishness, fear, narrowmindedness etc. From the stage of devotion, thus, a person enters the region which is reached by a man of jñāna, too, after great self-restraint and mental conflict. The Bhāgavata aims at bringing revolution in human mind. It makes a bold attempt to turn the selfish, and ego-ridden human life of human beings in an instance of supreme dedication. When one tries to do everything for the Lord, how there can be any chance of personal downfall or spiritual degradation? In fact a God-fearing, devotion-intoxicated man is the biggest source of spiritual progress and social upliftment. The history bears a brilliant testimony to the fact that the number of the men of knowledge has been far less as compared with the number of the men of devotion and it is the latter who bore the torch of human culture in the best humanitarian spirit. It is also evident that the path of knowledge cannot be acceptable to a great majority of humanity because of their psychological reasons. But the touch of devotion is able to transform many a life in a miraculous manner. And these devotion lovers have brought sanity, satisfaction, and prosperity to human community. Vālmīki and Vyāsa, Kālīdāsa and Māgha, Sūradāsa and Tulasīdāsa, Vidyapati and Tagore, Ramakrishna Paramahamsa and Vivekanand, Gandhi and Vinoba, Aurbindo and Radhakrishnan and all other illustrious sons of humanity were fed on devotion and led on the path of nobility and chastity, paving the way for the real progress of human society.

I have established in my work that won the degree of the Ph. D. for me that the Bhāgavata at least in its kernel form is very old. It is not desirable and opportune to restate all the arguments establishing this fact here. What is important to note is the conclusion drawn after a lengthy examination of the question of the date of the Bhāgavata, which runs as follows:

"We conclude then that far from being the work of one Bopadeva in the 13th century, the Bhāgavata is probably the product of the 9th century B.C.. When I say that it is the product of pre-Christian era. I do not mean that it existed in its present form in that distant past; but the kernel of the work was definitely composed at that time."[162]

I am sure that my conclusion is quite correct and therefore, it is but natural to expect that the Bhāgavata did influence the subsequent thinkers, notably Śaṅkara [163], Rāmānuja,[164] and Vallabha.[165]

In fact the Bhāgavata influenced many saints, seers, and mystics, along with the common men. The upsurge of bhakti that took India by storm and is still the life-blood of her culture and civilization, has been engendered by the Bhagavadgītā and the Bhāgavata. Kabīr, Mīrā, Sūradāsa, Tulāsīdāsa and a host of others bear a living testimony to this fact.

References

1. The work is being published by M/s Munshi Ram Manohar Lal, Delhi.
   Vide its first chapter.
2. Vide Appendix to my thesis, referred to above.
3. Bhā. 2-9-32.
4. Bhā. 2-6-39.
5. Bhā. 1-2-11.
6. "In the root divine Wisdom is all-Brahman; in the stem she is all Illusion; in the flower she is all World; and in the fruit all Liberation." Tattva Tantra (quoted from The Perennial Philosophy, p. 77).
   bṛhatvād bṛhanatvācca tad brahmetyābhidhīyate. Viṣṇu P.
   "Brahma implies an all-pervading, omnipotent, bigger than the biggest power." (Dr. Janardan Mishra-Bhāratiya Pratika Vidya, Rashtrabhasha Parishad, Sammelan Bhavan, Patna, 1959, p. 3-4).

aiśvarasya samagrasya, dharmasya yaśasaḥ śriyaḥ
vairāgyasya atha mokṣasya ṣnnāṁ bhaga itīraṇā. i.e.

the term 'bhagavan' stands for one possessing supreme majesty, dharma (dutifulness), renown, beauty, renunication and liberation.

The term Īśvara stands for a power that can turn the humanly impossible thing into possible : kartumakartumanyathā kartum samartha:

There is still another sense of the term 'bhagavān' :

utpattim ca vināśaṁ ca bhūtānamagatiṁ gatin.
vetti vidyāmavidyaṁ ca sa vacyo bhagavāniti i.e.

a power which knows the origin,destruction, good or bad state of the beings and is aware of vidyā i.e. real knowledge as well as avidya i.e. the false knowledge, is called 'bhagavān'.

7. Bhā. 5-12-11.
8. Bhā. 3-32-26.
9. Bhā. 2-4-21.
10. Bhā. 10-8-15.
11. Bhā. 10-14-4.
12. Bha. 4-11-23; 10-87-15.
13. Bhā 8-1-11; 8-3-24; 1-3-35.
14. do 7-9-49
15. do 10-40-4 to 10.
16. do 7-9-48; 6-9-37, 38; 10-20-4; 7-9-48.
17. do 10-20-4.
18. Vide Brahma Sūtra 1-1-22 (Śaṅkara); and 2-1-33.
19. Bhā. 7-9-44; 21-12, 13.

Tulasīdāsa has specifically stated that there is no religion higher than serving the others:

'parahita sarisa dharama nahi bhāī
para pīḍā sama adhamāī.'

20. In this context the cases of literary giants like Tulasīdāsa, Sūradāsa, Tolstoy, Shakespeare, Tagore etc. can be remembered.
21. Bhā. 2-7-51, 52.
22. do 1-2-6.
23. do 1-2-8.
24. do 1-2-14,
25. do 2-1-5.
26. do 2-2-33

27. do 2-2-34, 36
28. do 2-1-6.
29. do 3-25-44
30. do 4-29-49.
31. do 4-29-50.
32. do 4-31-9.
33. do 4-31-14.
34. do 6-3-22.
35. do 7-7-55.
36. do 3-24.43.
37. do 5-3-2.
38. do 6-4-33, 34.
39. do 7-9-27.
40. do 3-9-4.
41. do 3-9-23.
42. do 6-9-33.
43. do 7-6-23.
44. do 8-1-16.
45. do 8-3-17.
46. do 10,-27-6.
47. do 10-29-41
48. do 10-32-2.
49. do 1o-37-31.
50. do 10-38-36.
51. do 10-38-22; 10-72-6.
52. do 10-39-55.
53. do 10-64-26.
54. do 11-1-6.
55. do 11-7-18.
56. do kṛṣṇastu bhagavān svayaṁ Bhā. 1-3-28; 1-7-7; 10-44-13.
57. The Bhāgavata Māhātmya as contained in the Padma Purāṇa 1-11.
58. Bhā. 6-2-18. The Story of Ajāmila is instructive. (6-1).
59. Bhā. 11-2-33.
60. do 11-2-42.
61. Bhāgavata Māhātmya (Padma Purāṇa), 1-45.
62. do 2-18.
63. do 2-71.

64. Bha. 1-12-30.
65. Bhāgavata Māhātmya (Padma Purāṇa), 5-65.
66. do do do ,6-82.
67. Bhā. 10-29-31.
68. do 11-2-36.
69. do 10-44-15.
70. do 1-2-6.
71. do 11-27-53.
72. do 11-14-14; 3-29-13.
73. do 11-14-17.
74. do 11-12-15.
75. do 10-47-66.
76. do 10-47-67. Uddhava wanted to become even the creepers of Vṛndāvana. (10-47-61).

    Another poet devotee Rasakhāna expressed his desire to be a cowherd of Gokula if he were to be born as a human being. If he were to be born as an animal, then he would like to be a cow of Nanda. If he were to become a stone, he would like to be a part of the mountain Govardhana; and if he were to be born as a bird, he would like to reside on the branches of Kadama tree by the side of the river Kālīndī (the Yamunā):

    mānusa hau to vahi rasakhāna basaun saṅga gokula gāvn ke gwārana:

    jau pasu hau tau kahā basu merau caraun nita naṅda kī dhenu maṅjhārana;

    pāhana hau to vahī giri ko jo kiyo hari chatra puraṇdara dhrāna;
    jau khaga hau to basero karau mili kālīndī phoola kadaṁba ki dārana.

77. Bhā. 6-12-22.
78. do 7-9-10.
79. 'priyasya pratirūḍha mūrtayaḥ' —Bhā. 10-30-3.
80. Bhā. 1-1-2.
81. Bhā. 2-4-19; 7-9-10.
82. do 11-11-29 to 33.
83. Bhā. 8-1-10.
84. do 2-1-5; 2-2-36.
85. do 1-2-14.
86. do 10-86-46.
87. do 10-10-38.

88. Bhā. 3-27-21 to 23.
89. do 7-5-23.
90. do 2-3-19 to 24.
90. (1) do 9-4-18 to 20.
91. do 7-7-29.
92. do 7-7-30 to 36.
93. do 11-29-9 to 16.
94. do 11-19-20 to 23.
95. do 3-27-6 to 11.
96. do 4-22-22 to25.
97. do 3-29-15 to 19.
98. do 11-11-34 to 41.
99. do 3-28-2 to 6.
100. do 5-5-10 to 13.
101. do 7-11-8 to 12.
102 do 11-3-23 to 31.
103. do 3-29-7 to 13.
104. do 10-30-3.
105. The Bhāgvata (Māhātmya (Padma Purāṇa), 1-45.
Bhā. 12-13-18.
106. do 11-20-6; vide Śrīkṛṣṇa' address to Gopikās : 10-82-47.
do 1-7-10; 12-12-4.
107. do 7-9-11.
108. do 1-1-1.
109. do 4-28-62; 11-3-53.
110. do 7-9-51.
111. do 3-29-26.
112. do 3-29-25; 3-29-21.
113. do 10-55-44.
114. do 10-86-55.
115. do XI-27.
116. do 11-27-12.
117. do 11-27-7.
118. do 11-27-15, 8.
119. do 11-27-17.
120. do 11-27-23.
121. do 11-29-34.
122. do 11-29-32.

123. Talks on the Gītā, by Acharya Vonoba Bhave, Akhil Bharat Sarva Seva Sangha Prakashan, Kashi, 859, p. 174-175.
124. Bhā. 1-2-11; 1-3-28; 1-22-8,29; 7-10-49; 10-1-3; 10-12-11.
125. do 10-47-46.
126. do X-40.
127. do X-2, X-14, X-27.
128. do 2-1-9; 10-87-1; 10-87-15.
129. do 11-3-35 to 40.
130. do 2-9-32.
131. R.V. X-29.
132. Bṛhadāraṇyaka 5-1-1; Īśa Upaniṣad-Śānti Pāṭha.
133. R.V. X-90.
134. Chapter XI.
135. II-i-4,9.
136. III-14.
137. Bhā, 2-6-15; 2-1-23 to 37.
138. do 4-22-37.
139. 'Is Vedānta the Future Religion ?', Advaita Ashram, Mayavati, Almora, 1951, p. 30.
140. Vinoba, Talks on the Gītā, p. 167.
141. The Bhāgavata Māhatmya (Padma Purāṇa), 3-58.
142. Bhā. 7-9-48; 8-6-11; 10-20-4.
143. do 2-1-9.
144. do 1-1-1.
145. do 12-13-1.
146. do 12-13-15.
147. do 12-13-18.
148. do 12-13-19.
149. do 1-1-17, 18; 1-11-35; 2-4-7; 3-26-4; 6-9-26; 10-40-10.
150. do IV-III-14.
151. Bhā. 1-3-36.
152. do 1-9-32.
153. do 2-4-7.
154. do 10 40-10.
155. Cultural Heritage of India, Vol. III, pp. 288-9.
156. Bhā. 3-7-2 to 7.
157. Apte's The Practical Sanskrit English Dictionary, third Edition, p, 817.
158. Bhā. 5-19-5.

159. yadeva paramaṁ brhma sarvato'pi bṛhattamam
sarvasyāpi bṛhmaṇatvāt kṛṣṇa ityabhidhīyate.

doṣān kṛṣati nivārayatīti kṛṣṇah. vide Bhā. 10-10-33 etc.

The Bhāgavata has tried to interpret the various weapons and ornaments worn by Srikṛṣṇa in an allegorical manner. (vide XII-11). The Bhāgavata has left no opportunity of reminding readers that Śrikṛṣṇa is not a human being that was loved. He is the Absolute Himself. (7-15-79, 10-1-23, 10-3-31 etc.

'kṛṣṇo vai paramaṁ daivatam' declares the Gopālapūrvatāpinyupaniṣad.

vide Bhā. 2-7-47; 4-9-13; 4-24-65; 5-3-4; 6-3-16; 8-1-11 etc.)

160. Bhā. 11-31-28.

161. do 12-12-4.

162. vide my thesis titled as "The Concepts of Iśvara, Prakṛti and Jīva in the Bhāgavata Purāṇa" submitted in September 1962 of the Agra University and approved for the degree of the Ph.D., p. 33.

163. According to Mādhvācārya's Bhāgavata-tātparya-nirṇaya Śaṅkara wrote a commentary on the Bhāgavata. (vide Kalyāṅa, Bhāgavatāṅka, varśa 16, aṅka 1, p. 57.

The commentry, however, is not presently available. But even in the absence of it, there is sufficient testimony that, point that the Bhāgavata did influence the mind of Śaṅkara.

164. Rāmānuja has also quoted from the Bhagavata in his work Vedāṅtatatvasāra. (vide the above mentioned Bhāgavatānka of the Kalyāna, p. 57).

165. Vallabha has shown his reverence for the Bhāgavata by calling it "samadhibhāṣā vyāsasya" in his Tatvadipanibaṅdha Sāstra,7-8.

4

Concept of devotion in the Bhagavadgītā

GOD MUST RULE THE HEART

"But He is no God who merely satisfies the intellect, if He ever does. God to be God must rule the heart and transform it. He must express Himself in every the smallest act of His votary. This can only be done through a definite realization more real than the five senses can ever perceive. Sense perceptions can be, often are, false and deceptive, however real they may appear to us. Where there is realization outside the senses, it is infallible. It is proved not by extraneous evidence, but in the transformed conduct and character of those who have felt the real presence of God within.

"Such testimony is to be found in the experience of an unbroken line of prophets and sages in all countries and climes. To reject this evidence is to deny oneself.

"This realization is preceded by an immovable faith. He who would in his own person test the fact of God's presence can do so by a living faith."

—Mahatma Gandhi

(From the book "God is Truth", pp. 18-19)

....

The Bhagavadgītā is a part of the great work, the Mahābhārata, which describes the story of the Pāṅdavas and the Kauravas. The Mahābhārata can be understood as an allegorical description of warring tendencies present in a person. Our tendencies are either good or bad, and there is conflict between the two at times. In this hour of fierce inner conflict our sense of discrimination shows us the right path. Arjuna, the chief character of the Pāṅdava family, was called Arjuna because he was essentially a person of purity (ārjava). Kauravas were the sons of Dhritarāshtra, a blind person. Hence, Kauravas represent our blind urges that represent the Id in the words of Freudian psychology. Pāṅdavas, on the other hand, represent the noble tendencies of the Ego and Kṛṣṇa represents the Super Ego. Human heart is the battle ground of these warring tendencies.

However, for an average Indian (Hindu) the Gītā is the teaching of the Supreme Himself. In fact, the Gītā is the only book in the world where we find a supreme teacher calling himself the God. The message delivered itself carries the stamp of a divine declaration because it is meant for every person and is most synthetic in character. It is impossible to come across another work in the world that can match well with the message of the Gītā. In India itself this work has been highly respected. The Mahābhārata states that the Gītā alone should be followed leaving away other scriptures because it has come straight from the mouth of God Himself. It has been hailed as the quintessence of the Upanishadic knowledge. Gandhi hailed the Gītā as his mother. In fact even in the domain of Indian philosophy, the Gītā occupied the highest place right from the time immemorial. It is an important book of the Prasthāna Trayī. Every Indian teacher of philosophy was required to write his commentary on the Gītā, the Brahma Sūtras and the principal Upanishads. Thus we find right from the great Shankara to Ramanuja, Vallabha, Madhva and Radhakrishnan every āchārya tried to write a commentary on this important work.

The Gītā contains lofty philosophical thought about the Supreme Truth. According to the Gītā, "It is the perceiver of all sense-objects, though devoid of all senses; though unattached and attributeless. It is the sustainer of all and enjoyer of the qualities (the three constituents of the Prakṛti). It is without and within all beings, and constitutes both animate and inanimate creation. By reason and its subtlety, It is incomprehensible; It is both at hand and far away. Though indivisible (like ether). It stands as if divided among beings. That knowable substance is the sustainer of beings (as Viṣṇu), destroyer (as Rudra), and creator (as Brahmā). The Light of lights, It is said to be beyond the darkness of māyā. It is Knowledge itself, as well as the object of knowledge, and is also worth attaining through knowledge. It is specially seated in the hearts of all." (XIII-14 to 17).

It is called the Supreme Person (Purushottama) by the Gītā (XV-18). The Gītā contains the most developed type of knowledge. On one side it states, "The Yogi, who is united in identity with all-pervading infinite consciousness, and looks on all with an equal eye, sees the Self present in all beings,and all beings existing in the Self" (VI-29) and on the other hand it states that a person of knowledge "sees all beings existing in God" (VI-30). The test of a man of realization is that he should see God everywhere (VII-19) The wise look with the same eye on a Brahmin endowed with learning and culture, a cow, an elephant, a dog, and a pariah." (V-18) But essentially the Gītā is a work that lays emphasis on the way of devotion.

"Neither by study of the Vedas, nor by penance, nor by charity, nor by rituals can I be seen in this form" (XI-53), asserts the Gītā. The Supreme can be realized only through single-minded devotion. (XI-54) "That Supreme Purusha in whom all beings reside, and by whom all this is pervaded, is attainable only by exclusive devotion." (VIII-22) "I am the source of all creation; everything in the world moves because of Me; knowing thus the wise full of devotion worships Me. With their mind fixed on Me, with their lives surrendered to Me, enlightening one another about My greatness and speaking of Me, they ever remain contented and take delight in Me.

On those ever united through meditation with Me and worshipping Me with love, I confer that Yoga of wisdom through which they attain Me." (X-8 to 10)

Unification with God through "supreme faith" is the most desirable thing. The Gītā is liberal enough to accept both the meditation on the unmanifest and immutable Brahman (Abstract Absoute) as well as meditation on the Manifest God as equally good. But it tries to add that the path of those who have their mind attached to the unmanifest is more difficult, because self-identification with the Unmanifest is attained with difficulty by those who are centred in the body. (XII-5)

But the condition is that the attachment to the Lord should be unflinching. Without such an unflinching devotion, it is not possible to attain the Lord. (XIII-11) But one who has this unflinching devotion for the Lord, is sure to transcend the three Guṇās and the world constituted by them and one rises to the topmost position of attainment of the highest state which is "the abode of the imperishable Brahma, of immortality, of everlasting virtue and of unending bliss." (XIV-26, 27).

The mark of a devotee is that he is completely attached to the Lord and all his acts are for His sake alone (IX-34). He cannot think about anything else but God. For him his Lord is the only thing in the world.

A devotee is free from pride and infatuation, he is not a slave of attachment and worldly desires, he has no traces of the pairs of opposites like pleasure and pain, and constantly dwells in God. (XI-5) He is free from malice towards all beings, is friendly as well as compassionate, is devoid of egoism, is forgiving by nature, treats pleasure and pain alike, is always contented, is the master of body, mind, senses, has firm resolution, and has surrendered his mind and intellect to the Lord. He is not a source of annoyance to the world, is never upset or offended by the world, is free from worldly pleasure and anger, perturbation and fear. He has no craving for any worldly object, is pure internally and externally, is not touched by any distractions, and renounces the feeling of doership in all acts.

He neither rejoices nor hates, nor grieves, nor desires, renounces both good and evil, and has complete devotion for the Lord.

He is alike to friend and foe, and to honour and ignomity, to heat and cold, pleasure and pain.

He takes praise and criticism alike, feels attached to contemplation and is content with whatever comes to him unasked. He has no attachment for home and possesses strong will.

In short he is a person of pious wisdom, faith and devotion. Such a person alone is a real devotee. (XII-13 to 20)

Lord declares in the Gītā :

Give me your whole heart,
Love and adore me,
Worship Me always,
Bow to me only;
And you will find Me;
This is my promise
Who love you dearly.

Lay down all duties
In Me, your refuge.
Fear no longer,
For I will save you,
From sin and from bondage. (XVIII, 65, 66)

The most precious thing found in a devotee is his unflinching faith. His faith is like "the light of a lamp in a windless place" which knows no flickering. It is a faith so certain that it shall never be shaken by the heaviest sorrow. The Gītā asserts : "The faith of every being is shaped to his own mental constitution. Faith constitutes the very being of man. Therefore whatever the nature of his faith, that verily he is" (XVII-3).

The Gītā distinguishes between Sātvika, Rājasika and Tāmasika types of faith and pleads for an inculcation of Sātvika faith. (XVII-4).

The Gītā divides devotees in four categories viz. the seekers of worldly objects, the sufferer, the seeker for knowledge, and the man of wisdom. (VII-16)

Persons have their different temperaments. One person may pray God for getting riches or status, other person, who is ill, may pray God for getting health, some other person may possess inquisitive mind that tries to know reality about God, and lastly there may be a person who has a vision of God and loves Him from the bottom of his heart.

According to the Gītā a person of knowledge is the best devotee of God (VII-17). For such a person of knowledge the Lord declares "He is verily My own Self", the highest honour that can be bestowed on knowledge. (VII-18) The Gītā has utmost respect for knowledge because "all actions without exception culminate in knowledge" (IV-33). There is nothing more pious than knowledge. In fact in the domain of learning the Lord is metaphysics (X-32).

But the Gītā insists that this lofty knowledge cannot be obtained without the grace of God. He can be realized only through devotion. Neither by the study of the Vedas, nor by charity, nor by ritual can the Lord be realized. Devotion alone leads to real knowledge. (XI-53, 54) "Through devotion he comes to know Me in reality, what I am and who I am," declares Lord. (XVIII-55) That Supreme Purusha in whom all beings reside, and by whom all this is pervaded, is attainable only through exclusive devotion. (VIII-22) If one tries to know the Supreme only through intellect, one is bound to be unsuccessful, because discursive reasoning only confounds a man and no decisive opinion is possible. (II-41) Hence the Lord declares that theUltimate Truth can be known only through devotional attitude. Devotion shall transform a person completely and he shall see the One everywhere.

Seeing all things equal
The enlightened may look
On the brahmin, learned and gentle,
On the cow, on the elephant,
On the dog, on the eater of dogs. (V-18)

No man is doomed, if he chooses to love God. One should lift oneself by one's own efforts and should not degrade oneself; for one's own self is one's friend and one's own self is one's enemy. One's own self is the friend of that soul by whom the lower self (viz. the mind, the senses etc.) has been conquered; on the other hand, the very self of him, who has not conquered his lower self, behaves inimically like one's own enemy. (VI-5, 6)

All mankind
Is born for perfection
And each shall attain it
Will he but follow
His nature's duty. (XVIII-45)

A person has to cast off his mundane being, his empirical ego to attain the bliss of his real being. Then one

. . . casts from him
Vanity, violence,
Pride, lust, anger,
And all his possessions,
Totally free
From the sense of ego
And tranquil of heart;
That man is ready
For oneness with Brahman. (XVIII-53)

Talking about such an enlightened devotee, the Gītā states

Absorbed in Brahman
He overcomes the world
Even here, alive in the world.
Brahman is one,
Changeless, untouched by evil;
What home have we but Him ?
The enlightened, the Brahman-abiding,
Calm-hearted, unbewildered,
Is neither elected by the pleasant
Nor saddened by the unpleasant.
His mind is dead
To the touch of the external;
It is alive
To the bliss of the Atman,
Because his heart knows Brahman
His happiness is for ever. (V-19-21)

And

All consumed
Are their imperfections,
Doubts are dispelled,
Their senses mastered,
Their every action
Is wed to the welfare
Of fellow-creatures;
Such are the seers
Who enter Brahman
And know nirvāṇa. (V-25)

Let us not forget

Only that yogi
Whose joy is inward,
Inward his peace,
And his vision inward,
Shall come to Brahman
And know nirvāṇa. (V-24)

Devotion destroys the ego, which is responsible for miseries of life. In this context the following wòrds of Ramkrishna Paramahamsa are worth noting.

"Some retain the sense of ego as 'the servant I' or 'the devotee I'—the sense Thou art the Lord, I am Thy child"—even after attaining samādhī. The 'I' of a devotee does no harm to any living creature. It is like a sword which, after touching the philosopher's stone, is turned to gold. The sword retains the same form, but it does not cut or injure anyone." (Kathamrta. vol. I. p 46) He further adds, "The dry leaves of the coconut tree drop off in the wind, leaving marks on the trunk; those marks only show that there were leaves there at one time. Similary, only the form or mark of ego is left in one who has reached God. Also his passions remain only as empty forms. He becomes simple and pure like a child." (Ibid, vol. I. p. 91).

"Saṁkara and spiritual teachers like him come down to the consciousness of 'ego' for the teaching and good of humanity. . . The bee buzzes until it alights in the heart of the flower. It becomes silent as soon as it begins to drink the honey. Then again, after it has drunk its fill, it makes a sweet humming sound." (Ibid, vol. III, p. 10).

"Few can stay long on the roof. Those who reach samādhī and attain Brahman return to the lower plane of consciousness and then realize that it is he who has become man and the universe. The singer cannot hold to the highest note very long. He comes down to the lower notes. Similarly, the man of realization comes back from the transcendental consciousness and perceives the world of relativity, and though he sees the world, he sees Brahman everywhere." (Ibid, vol. III, p.11). Thus a devotee is a completely transformed soul.

We must not forget that the Gītā preaches devotion for the Supreme, the Purushottama, not for any lesser deity. It declares:

The Lord is everywhere
And always perfect;
What does He care for man's sin
Or the righteousness of man ? (V-15)

The Gītā believes in the knowledge of the immutable, eternal, and timeless existence called Brahma-nirvāṇa. It does not advocate a study of this Ultimate Being through intellectual concepts. It persuades a devotee to have a direct vision of that Reality through the spiritualized consciousness.

Utterly quite
Made clean-of passion,
The mind of the Yogi
Knows that Brahman,
His bliss is the highest. (VI-27)

The existence of that Reality is beyond doubt.

"The unreal has no existence, and the real never ceases to be; the reality of both has thus been perceived by the seers of truth". "Know that to be imperishable, by which all this is pervaded; for none can bring about the destruction of this indestructible substance". (II-16, 17)

Real devotion is a kind of Samādhī in which a person is completely united with the Supreme. Writing about such samādhī, Ramakrishna Paramahamsa states:

"When one attains samadhi then alone comes the knowledge of Brahman, and one attains the vision of God. In that ecstatic realization, all thoughts cease, and one becomes perfectly silent. There is no power of speech left by which to express Brahman. For verily is beyond thought and speech." (Kathamrita. vol III, pp. 9-10).

The Gītā is not rigid about the manifest or unmanifest aspects of the Supreme. Both are real. But unmanifest Brahman cannot be easily accepted for devotion. Hence manifest aspect of Brahman, God should be resorted to for devotion. (XII-3 to 5).

But the whole discussion about the manifest and unmanifest Reality is merely academic. The following opinion of Ramakrishna on this crucial point is very reasonable.

"The jñānī, or one of philosophic mind, analyses the universe of the senses, saying 'Brahman is not this, not that', and gives up all worldliness. Thus does he reach the knowledge of

Brahman, just as the man who climbs a staircase leaves each step behind and so reaches the roof. But Vijñānī, who gains an intimate knowledge of him, has his consciousness extended. He knows that the roof and the steps are all made of the same substance. He who is realized as Brahman by the process of elimination is also realized as becoming man and the universe. The Vijñānī knows that he who is without attributes in one aspect is, in another aspect, the repository of all blessed attributes.

The true knower knows that he who is Brahman is the personal God; that he who is impersonal, attributeless, and beyond the guṇas, is again the personal God, the repository of all blessed qualities. Man, the universe, mind, intelligence, love, dispassion, knowledge these are the expression of his power and glory." (Kathamrita, vol. III, pp. 11)

The concept of Reality expounded in the Gītā is so sublime that the intellectual concepts of theism or pantheism fail to catch its real meaning. Only a person who has imbibed the spirit of Upanishadic philosophy can understand it.

Yogi Aurobindo has correctly described the nature of the Real of the Gītā in the following words:

". . . it is no shrinking and gingerly theism afraid of the world's contradictions, but one which sees God as the omniscient and omnipotent, the sole original Being, who manifests in himself all, whatever it may be, good and evil, pain and pleasure, light and darkness as stuff of his own existence, and governs himself what in himself he has manifested. Unaffected by its oppositions, unbound by his creation, exceeding, yet intimately related to this Nature and closely one with her creatures, their Spirit, Self, highest Soul, Lord, Lover Friend, Refuge, he is ever leading them from within them and from above through the mortal appearances of ignorance and suffering and sin and evil, ever leading each through his nature and all through universal nature towards a supreme light and bliss and immortality and transcendence. This is the fullness of the liberating knowledge.

It is a knowledge of the Divine within us and in the world and at the same time a transcendent Infinite. An Absolute who has become all that is by his divine Nature, his effective power of Spirit, he governs all from his transcendence. He is intimately present within every creature and their cause, ruler, director of all cosmic happenings and yet is he far too great, mighty and infinite to be limited by his creation." (Essays on the Gītā, second series p. 133).

Thus there is no contradiction in the unmanifest Absolute and the manifest God. Not only this, this God even takes avatāra or incarnation whenever the state of world demands so. "Whenever there is decline of righteousness, and unrighteousness is in the ascendent, I take my incarnation for the protection of the virtuous and the destruction of the evil-doer", declares the Lord. (IV-7,8). It is just proper that God does not remain indifferent to the worsening condition of the world He himself has created, and sets it in order. But Lord declares:

I am the birthless, the deathless,
Lord of all that breathes.
I seem to be born;
It is only seeming,
Only my māyā.
I am still master of my Prakriti,
The power that makes me. (IV-6)

He who knows the nature
Of my task and my holy birth
Is not reborn
When he leaves this body
He comes to me. (IV-9)

Thus devotion of the Gītā is not just a feeling; it is a higher kind of knowledge that gives vision of the supreme and fills the entire being of a devotee with an enthralling experience.

Quickly I come
To those who offer me
Every action,
Worship me only,
Their dearest delight,
With devotion undaunted. (XII-6)

GOD OF THE BHĀGAVATA

Since the Bhāgavata is the pivotal work of Bhakti, it will be worthwhile to know something about its concept of God.

The Bhāgavata is of the view that though we ascribe many names to God, He is really-speaking One, Non-dual Reality. He is the sole Truth, the only Truth of the universe. From the standpoint of the Ultimate Truth, the universe, as we see and feel it, does not exist at all. It is just a creation of our lack of knowledge. As the Supreme is the sole existing Reality, even our self is really-speaking the Supreme himself. Thus the Bhāgavata preaches the pure Vedāntic doctrine of the sole reality of the Absolute.

However, the Bhāgavata prefers to call that Absolute or Brahman as Śrikṛṣṇa. If we try to go deep, we find that the term 'Krishna' has an allegorical meaning too. It means that Supreme Truth that attracts our sense organs, or that rules our being. The Bhāgavata actually implies that Ultimate Being when it talks about Krishna. And lest we should forget this fact, many occasions are used to remind about this fact through various panegyrics addressed by deities or Brahma or the Vedas etc. The Bhāgavata clearly states that really-speaking the Absolute has neither any form nor any description. He is beyond all these.

But the outstanding feature of the Supreme, according to the Bhāgavata, is that He is enchantingly beautiful. He is the beautiful incarnate. Beauty has its universal attraction. Therefore the Bhāgavata depicted its Lord as exceedingly charming, although philosophically-speaking He is none else but the Absolute. Krishna has such beauty that the entire world is attracted towards Him. As a matter of fact the very term Krishna implies the universal attracter. The devotee who comes to Kṛṣṇa, first of all drawn by the irresistible charm of Kṛṣṇa, is able to achieve the supreme truth sooner or later, as by and by, his entire being is transformed due to his intense attachment for the Lord.

Though the Absolute is formless, by Māyā, His supreme power, He assumes any form so that his devotees may draw an inspiration from His presence. By Māyā, that Supreme undertakes the work of creating, protecting and destroying the universe.

This action of the Supreme has been termed Līlā by the Bhāgavata. Līlā means divine play, i.e. it is an effortless and undirected act of God. Play also implies an exuberance of energy. The whole world is thus a play of God, because there is no better way of describing this divine creation. The entire Līlā of Kṛṣṇa admits of an allegorical explanation. In fact the Gopalapūrvātāpaniyopanishad has interpreted the entire Līlā of Kṛṣṇa allegorically alone.

The Bhāgavata has brought the Absolute nature of the Kṛṣṇa by using adjectives indicating qualitylessness e.g. nirguṇa, anādi etc.; by describing the state before creation; by suggesting that He is beyond description even by Shankara, Brahma etc.; and by calling Him Praṇava or the mystic sign called AUM.

God assumes embodied form as the worship of the Formless and the Qualityless is difficult for an ordinary person. Avtāra carries the distinct meaning of the Supreme's descending to a level where a layman can find sufficient glory in Him to follow Him willingly and spontaneously. Saguṇa is therefore necessary for a beginner. However, as the knowledge grows, the Saguṇa aspect disappears and the Nirguṇa aspect of God is revealed like the rainbow which ultimately disappears in the sky. Rainbow is the symbol of the Saguṇa while the sky is the symbol of the Nirguṇa.

When this basic philosophy of the Bhāgavata is not understood by a person of less intelligence, he is likely to misunderstand the various līlās of Kṛṣṇa like the Rāsa-līlā. He forgets that the only motive behind the mind of the author of the Bhāgavata is to attract the mind of an average person towards the Supreme in a loveable manner.

The popularity of the Bhakti movement is a clear indication that this method of drawing the mind of a person towards the Truth has succeeded immensely.

Human beings have three basic tendencies which can be called cognition, conation and affection. When the cognitive tendency becomes dominant, a person worships the formless aspect of Godhood; when conative tendency becomes powerful, he attaches utmost importance to the rituals and tries to please Viṣṇu, Śiva or any other deity through a ritualistic approach; but when the affective tendencies become dominant, a person loves the Supreme in the form of an incarnation etc. whole-heartedly. The questions of knowledge and ceremonies are not so significant for him. To appeal to these respective tendencies, the Bhāgavata has depicted God in three different ways. But at the same time care has been taken to see that these three are not considered separate. Thus for the Bhāgavata, Kṛṣṇa is Infinite, God and Avatāra all rolled in one. Let a person see the Supreme in the light of his dominant tendency. Unless the Supreme has these triune aspects, He cannot satisfy each and every type of human being. The merit of this unique approach lies in the fact that even the lowliest can be brought on the level of the best in course of time and the monopoly of the people of knowledge can be destroyed.

Human beings have by nature great fascination for beauty. Beauty attracts human minds like a magnate attracts pieces of iron. The Bhāgavata is fully alive to this fact. That is why Śrīkṛṣṇa has been depicted as infinitely charming. Attracted by this charm, human beings come closer to Him and ultimately they become transformed souls.

The Bhāgavata is, however, emphatic in asserting that the Supreme is formless and the world of plurality is unreal from the standpoint of the ultimate truth; it at the same time puts its view in a very psychologically sound way. It gives due importance to the natural urges of man, because no man can go against them. What is needed is to transform them gradually till the highest point of truth is reached.

That is why the universe has not been called a mirage or illusion. It has been called a līlā or divine play. The universe is thus the produce of celestial mirth and gaity. One has to understand this fact. Once we understand this truth, we shall develop a tendency of non-attachment to the world; for we are all playing a play, we all being essentially the Absolute. After this attitude of non-attachment, the next step of treating this world of diversity and multiplicity as unsubstantial follows logically.

The apparent plurality is just a fiction of our ignorant mind, if we view the world from the standpoint of ultimate reality. Thus we find that the Bhāgavata has invented a very effective instrument of reconciling the duty of the world (for every player has some duty to perform) with the metaphysical truth of non-dualism. We need not discard this universe, for it is the play of the Supreme. What is needed is simply the recognition of the fact that we should not think ourselves bound by the shackles of misery and pangs, unhappiness and sorrows; for this goes against our basic nature of sheer bliss, knowledge and consciousness.

The Bhāgavata has tried to make this point lucid through many symbolic stories like the Puranjana Upākhyāna.

Thus we find that philosophically speaking, the cult of devotion subscribes to the philosophy of non-dualism. It accepts multiplicity in the beginning. But it proceeds to add that this multiplicity is only apparent. We must transcend it and reach the abode of non-dualistic truth. This has to be done through the pathway of devotion which transforms our innate urges.

Philosophically speaking, there can be only two possible positions so far as the relation between the Ultimate Reality and the embodied self (jiva) is concerned. Without entering into the question whether the Reality is one and non-dual or two or many, we can presume that the Realty is one and non-dual.

Śaṅkara has declared that the only true view is that the Brahman alone is real, the universe of multiplicity is an illusion, and there is no difference between the Ātman (the Real) and the self. "The Self is not a thing unknown to anybody at any time, not a thing to be reached (attained) or got rid of, or acquired.

"Just as there is no need for any external evidence to know one's own body, so also there is no need for any external evidence to know one's Self which is nearer than the body. So, for the wise, practice of Jnana is equally well known automatically.

"The process of valid knowledge is dependent on Atman (the knower). So Atman has to be posited before the process of knowledge commences.

"An object of knowledge is apprehended through cognition; so cognition is automatically known as pleasure and the like.

"Atman (the Self) is Brahman.

"It is one without a second; it is no object (of any of our senses); it is the very Self. So it is right to say that this (entity to be known) cannot be expressed or described by words.

"Having no form etc., this thing (the Self) is not an object of direct perception by any sense and, not possessing any indicative mark it does not become a subject of inference.

"It is not proper to state that the Jiva is different from Ishvara (the Lord.)

"Brahman is not, we reply, non-objective in the absolute sense. For Brahman is the object of the ego-idea. We know quite well, by intuition, that the inner Self must exist, since the ego-idea is a presentation of the Self. Nor is it an absolute rule that objects can be superimposed only upon such other forms as are placed before us; for ignorant people superimpose a dark blue colour upon the Sky, which is not an object of sense perception."

Thus Śaṅkara has tried to prove that the Brahman alone is true and real.

Though generally it has been believed that devotion needs a duality of the object of devotion and the devotee, yet it should be remembered that even the important works of devotion like the Bhāgavata believe that ultimately only the Lord is real. This implies that the duality and multiplicity are found only on the empirical level. But even Śaṅkara has stated that the world has empirical existence.

The very first verse of the Bhāgavata tells us that the great Truth is the Absolute alone. Kunti tells us that this Truth is hidden by the cover of Māyā and the people of low intelligence cannot recognise the Supreme (1-8-19). The Supreme has been described as indeterminate (nirguṇa) and nondual (advayaṁ) by the Bhāgavata. (II-vi-39). Even at the end, the Bhāgavata declares its faith in the Supreme Truth alone (XII-xiii-19). Really speaking, this very Supreme has been accepted in the form of Śrīkṛṣṇa, because the latter form of the Supreme appears as full of enchantment and sweetness (IX-xxii-64).

The path of devotion is not engaged in the enquiry of the ultimate nature of the Supreme. It starts with the presupposed opinion that the object of a devotee's desire is the Ultimate reality. It only tries to realize that ideal object of their devotion through devoted attachment. This will be clear from the account found in the Bhakti sūtras like Nārada Bhakti Sūtras and Śāṇdilya Sūtras.

The Śāndilya Sūtra is quite clear on this point. The Sutra no. 29 states "Kāśyapa thinks her (the understanding), (as) absorbed in the majesty and the lordliness of the Deity, (to be the cause of final emancipation), on account of the supremacy (of the Lord over Men). Human souls must first know the Supreme before they can know themselves. And Kāśyapa represents the view that Brahman and Jīva (God and man) are eternally distinct from each other.

The Śāṇdilya Sūtra thereafter proceeds to state in the Sūtra no. 30 "Badarayana (thinks the understanding), (When) absorbed soley in Atman, (to be the cause of final emancipation)."

Here the non-dualistic concept of relation between the Ātman and the jīva is indicated according to which the Ātman alone exists, and multiplicity is the creation of Māyā. The Vedānta Sūtra (IV. I. 3) clearly proclaims "They know moreover that all is Ātman and they are solely devoted to and absorbed in it."

The Śāṇdilya Sūtra then proceeds to add in the Sutra no.31 that both these views can be synthesized. It states :

'Śāṇḍilya (regards understanding, when) deeply absorbed in both, (to be the cause of emancipation), from the authority of the Vedas and from valid arguments."

Testimony (Sabda) is a respected source of knowledge in Indian philosophy. And the Vedic testimony declares "From Brahman, the originator of sacrifices, the Ṛg Veda and the Sama Veda and the Yajurveda and all verses came out."

The Chāndogya Upanishad further states "Verily all this is Brahman, for all this is born of It and disappears in it. It should be worshipped with a calm and equipoised mind. . . . This my self within the heart is that Brahman; (let one meditate upon Him thus): when departing from this body I shall reach Him. He who has devotion verily (reaches Him). There is no doubt in it." (III. 14. 1-4).

Having proved his point through the testimony, Kāśyapa asserts that the matter can be proved even through logical arguments. But as can be imagined even these arguments are rooted in testimony. The Vedic testimony declares that the Brahman is possessed of supreme powers and majesty and is the very self of Jīva. Thus the Taittirīya Upanishad declares that Brahman is that Supreme Reality "Whence all these beings are created, in whom all the creation lives and moves and has its being, where all goes and wherein all disappears." (III. 2.2.)

The Bhagavadgītā too declares this truth when it states "An eternal portion of Mine having become an individual soul in the world of life" (XV. 7).

Thus it is clear that the Jīvas are in fact the Brahman. Even the process of devotion establishes this very fact. In the beginning there is a duality of the subject of devotion and the devotee. But when devotion reaches maturity, there is identity of the subject of devotion (ārādhya) and the devotee (ārādhaka) as is clear from the cases of milkmaids of Vṛja who became the very Kṛṣṇa. (priyasya pratirūḍha mūrtayaḥ).

Hence duality is present only in the beginning. It melts away into a unity ultimately.

A second argument too can be adduced. The Sāṇḍilya Sūtra no. 39 declares that Brahman and Māyā or Prakṛti are mutually dependent. And both are ever united, as per sūtra no. 41, because both are without beginning. Hence, how can the jivas or nature can be separated from the Supreme ?

It should not be forgotten that Śrīkṛṣṇa or Rāma or Śiva or any other form of the Lord is essentially Brahman as is clear from the Sūtra no. 53.

The Sūtra no.93 specifically asserts that "multiplicity or unity appears on account of the presence of absence of upādhi or limitations like the sun."

The Viṣṇu Purāṇa tells us "As the one sky appears to be many according to the difference of colours, white, blue etc., so does the one self appear to be many to the erring eyes." (II. xvi. 12).

Therefore even the philosophy of devotion agrees with the statement of the Chāndogya. "All this indeed is Brahman" (III. xiv.1) and the declaration of the Kaṭha Upanishad "Multiplicity there is none here." (IV.II).

When the Upādhi of jīva is destroyed, with the dawn of real devotion, the oneness of the Lord (Brahman) is realized, much like the sun, the source of light, which appears to be many on account of the intervention of the mirrors, but shines forth as one when the mirrors are removed.

That is why the Nārada Bhakti Sūtra states in the sūtra no.33 "the path of devotion should be adopted, to the exclusion of the others, by those who desire salvation."

The Sūtra no.74 of the Nārada Bhakti Sūtra that is why declares "Vain discussion should not be undertaken." When there is only one Reality, why there should be any discussion at all? Those persons, who believe in multiplicity or duality may quarrel or enter into disputations, but a person having faith in the existence of one Lord alone and united with Him through proper devotion has neither a tendency nor a necessity to waste time and energy in such vain discussions.

Devotion gives undisturbed peace and yields highest ecstasy (Nārada Bhakti Sūtra 60).

Such a devotee overcomes all limitations; and still further helps mankind to overcome their limitations. (Nārada Sūtra 50).

The Śāṇdilya Sūtra very emphatically states "There is only one Self and not many selves, from the standpoint of ultimate reality." (Sūtra 93) And yet there is a difference between a Jīva and Brahman at the empirical level. A Jīva is characterised by limitations and accidents while Brahman is free from them. (Sūtra 35).

It has been made clear by the Śāṇdilya Sūtra that this world is not going to end, probably because māyā is a power whose power is supreme so long as the Lord prefers to indulge into His divine play called Līlā. Hence there shall always be some Jīvas who shall be misguided by their lower tendencies, and Lord's grace shall be needed for their salvation. (Sūtra 36).

The universe too is not unreal so far as the divine play lasts. Of course, the Lord cannot be influenced by Prakṛti or nature which is the material cause of the universe. Prakṛti is subservient to the Lord. The Supreme is the creator of Māyā, hence how can He be a creation of Māyā ? The Lord remains immutable like the implements, sticks etc. in the preparation of earthen jars. (Sūtra 37).

Thus it is evident that even according to the standard tenets of devotion, devotion is based on the sound and solid rock of the Advaita philosophy. Of course, we do not find a systematic exposition of this philosophy, because there is no necessity for that.

Devotion and Knowledge

To understand the relation between the Vedānta and devotion, we can try to acquaint ourselves with the relationship existing between devotion and knowledge. Important thinkers of the Bhakti philosophy have always accepted that there is a close connection between knowledge and devotion. The Bhāgavata Purāṇa which is the most authoritative work on devotion has stated, "It is the quintessence of the Vedānta philosophy. He who has tasted its nectar-like juice will not be atracted by anything else. (XII-xiii-15).

Nārada Bhakti Sūtra states "When adored with love the Supreme speedily manifests himself and gives his devotees perception." (Śūtra 80). Saṅkara has defined devotion as knowledge of the supreme reality, Ātman or (Brahman paramārthajñānalakṣāṇa) and considers it essential for the attainment of the Supreme. He himself wrote devotional hymns in praise of different aspects of the Godhead like Bhavānī, Viṣṇu and Śiva. He addresses Bhavāni "You alone are my refuge (gatis tvaṁ gatis tvaṁ tvaṁ eka bhavānī). Madhusūdana Sarasvatī, who was a great exponent and advocate of the Vedānta philosophy, writes "I know not what truth there is beyond Kṛṣṇa." Ānandagiri has expressed the opinion that ripening of meditation on God or Brahman conditioned by Māyā if practised repeatedly for a long time produces a desire in the mind of a person to know the nature of Brahman unconditioned by Māyā and ultimately it culminates in the experience of Supreme. (Sopādḥikābhidhyāna-paripāken nirupādhikaṁ anusandadhāndsya tattvasākṣātkāra-sambhavāt—Ānandagiri's gloss on the Saṅkara's Bhāṣya on the Bhagavangītā, xii, 20).

Mahādevananda Sarasvatī also holds the view that meditation on God produces trance in which a devotee seeks an identity with the Ultimate Reality. (Advaitacintākaustubha).

The Advaita thinkers are of the opinion that devotion purifies mind from the worldly attachments and impurities and ultimately helps a person in realizing his identity with the Lord. (Madhusūdana's commentary on the Bhagavadgītā ii,6-6; ix, 34).

Rāmānuja also holds a view that devotion is not something quite different from knowledge. On the other hand, devotion is the culmination of true knowledge. (Bhaktyeva bhagavadjñānaṁ). In fact it has been accepted by the devotees that even the idea of the Advaita (nondual reality, dawns on the mind of a person due to the grace of the Supreme (Īśvarānugrahādeva puṅsāṁadvaitavāsanā). The Viṣṇu Pūrāṇa, which is an accepted work on devotion, clearly states that Yoga is essentially conjuction of the mental tendency with the Supreme i.e. the mind is merged in the infinite.

(Ātmaprayatnasāpeksā viśiṣṭā yā manogatiḥ
tasyā brahmaṇi sanyogo yoga ityabhidhīyate. 6-7-31).

Even the Gopis of Vṛja, who are the best examples of devotion, were not driven to Kṛṣṇa merely out of a blind attachment. They knew that he is the great Seer and not a mere child of Yasoda and was born for the protection of the universe. (Bhāgavata 10-31-4). The Śāndilya Sūtra, therefore, is right when it states that Brahma Kānda is meant for devotion. (Sūtra 26) Svapaneśvara has declared that knowledge is the nearmost instrument means of devotion. (tatrāntaraṅgāśadhanaṁ jñānam)

Tulsīdāsa in his immortal work the Rāmacaritamānasa declares that there is no difference between devotion and knowledge (bhagatihi gyānahi nahi kachu bhedā).

A person has to perform all his actions till he is able to get that devotion which comes through ripe knowledge. When husk is separated from rice, where is the need of threshing it ?

The Śaiva thinkers too hold this very view. For example Rāmakaṇṭha has defined devotion as the immediate experience of Brahman.

(matsvarūpānubhavarūpam parāṁ kāṣthām adhirūḍhā bhaktireva vijñānam-Commentary on the Bhagavadgita ix-23).

On other occasion, he says that devotion is meditation on the nature of Ātman, which is nondual pure consciousness. (bhaktirevādvaya-cinmātra-svarūpa-brahma- tattva- bhāvanaya ātmana evopāsanam-Ibid ix-7). The characteristic feature of devotion is the complete absorption of a person in the Brahman. (Ibid xxiii, 65).

Kaundinya accepts devotion as meditation. (bhaktir bhavana-Pañcarāthrabhāṣy, ii, 20). The Pāṣupasūtra states that a devotee should have undivided devotion to Siva, the Lord, and meditate on Him while sitting, walking, lying, waking, or dreaming, if he seeks union with the Supreme. (ii, 20)

The celebrated work, the Bhagavadgītā declares that a person having faith attains knowledge. (śṛaddhāvān labhate jṇānaṁ IV-39) It clearly implies that even knowledge can be obtained only through the gateway of devotion.

Mind is the most important factor in release and bondage. (mana eva manuṣyāṇāṃ kāraṇaṁ bandhamokṣayoḥ—(Brhannāradīya Purāṇa 1-47-4). Unless the attachment for the world and worldly objects is obliterated from the surface of mind, no release is possible. The Bhagavadgītā has clearly stated that mind is the sole factor that causes mundane attachments and affections. (II, 62-63) Once this bond of attachment is destroyed, the Truth dawns upon the mind. In the words of the Muṇḍaka Upanishad, the knots of the heart are broken, all doubts removed, and bondage of actions cut off, once this Truth is realized. (III-2) And mind can be transformed only through devotion. A verbal knowledge cannot destroy our ignorance, according to Tualsīdāsa. Just as the talk of a small lamp lying in a house cannot destroy the mass of darkness enveloping the house, in the same manner, it is not possible to destroy our ignorance through verbal knowledge.

(vākya gyāna atyanta nipuna, bhava pāra na pavai koi
nisi graha madhya dīpa ki bātanha tama nivṛtta nahi hohai)

On the other hand, once real devotion is accepted, a person becomes a completely transformed man. Then whatever action is done by a person, that becomes a worship of Lord.

(yad yad karma karomi tat tadaknilaṁ Saṁbhoḥ tavārādhanaṁ-Śiva Mahimna Stotra).

Salvation (mukti) is the return of the worldly Jīva i.e. the Jīva undergoing revolutions of births and deaths in ever-changing states of existences, into the state of Brahman who is pure existence, pure consciousness and pure bliss. According to the Nārada Bhakti Sūtra (no. 98) the very cause of the world is want of devotion. The fire of devotion burns down the sense of egoity present in the self, it destroys the sense of separate personality, the idea of the 'I', which is the real cause of worldly existence. As a result of this transformation, the self attains a state of perfect contentment, fullness of personality and absolute identification with the Infinite. On the other hand, want of devotion implies continuation of the delimting principle of ego, ahaṁkāra and the agentship in the performance of acts for the realization of intended ends, feelings, desires, volitions, attraction, repulsion, sense of success, sense of failure, pleasure, pain etc., which are responsible for rebirth of a self. Hence the Nārada Bhakti Sūtra (no. 96) asserts that devotion alone can destroy the bond of birth and rebirth.

The devotees seek liberation even in their life, because their minds are no longer affected by affections and desires. And when their Adṛṣṭam (the potential after effects of acts performed voluntarily) is destroyed, they become finally liberated. Thus that very effect which is realized through knowledge, can be realized through devotion.

A devoted soul cries :

"Shyam O Ghanashyam
You have like a fisherman cast your
net in the narrows
Of my mind
And towards you my thoughts
today
Must race like enchanted fish."

(Kamala Das in her poem Ghanshyam)

Or again as Kamala Das writes in her poem 'Radha'

"The long waiting
Had made their bond so chaste,
and all the doubting
And reasoning
So that in his first true embrace, she was girl
And virgin crying
Everything in me
Is melting, even the hardness at the core
O Krishna, I am melting, melting, melting
Nothing remains but
you. ."

Thus devotion takes a soul to her highest destination of unification with the Supreme.

5

Bhakti and some Men of Knowledge

"If Śaṁkara regards intellect as not the highest mode of man's consciousness, it is because the completed world of intellect still leaves us with a riddle. The completed world of logic is not the completed world of life and experience."

—Radhakrishan in
Indian Philosophy, Vol. II, 1927
pp. 523-24

Mokṣakāraṇasāmagryāṁ bhaktireva garīyasī
—Vivekacūḍāmaṇi, v. 32

Satyapi bhedāpagame nātha tavāhaṁ na māmakīnastvam;
Sāmudro hi taraṅgaḥ kvacana samudro na tāraṅgaḥ
Ṣaṭpadīstotram, v. 3

Gadī śaṁhhī cakrī vimalavanamālī sthirarucih
śaraṇyo lokeśo mama bhavatu kṛṣṇo 'kṣiviṣayaḥ.
—Kṛṣṇāṣṭakam, v. 1

Akhilabhuvanajanmasthemabhaṅgādilīle
vinatavividhabhutavrātarakṣaikadīkṣe;
śrutiśirasi vidīpte brahmaṇi śrīnivāse
bhavatu mama parasmin śemuṣī bhaktirūpā

—Maṅgala Śloka of the
Śri-bhāṣya

Bhaktiśca jñānaviśeṣa eva sarvamupapannam

—Vedārtha Saṁgraha, p. 252

Ananyaśaraṇaḥ tvatpādāravindayugalaṁ śaraṇāmahaṁ prapadye.

—Saraṇāgatigadyam, p. 5

Kṛṣṇātparaṁ nāsti daivaṁ vastu doṣavivarjitam.

—Antaḥkaraṇa-prabodha, v.1

Sarvadā sarvabhāvena bhajanīyo vṛjādhipaḥ.

—Catuḥślokī, v.1

Tasmātsarvaṁ parityajya dṛḍhavisvāsato hariṁ
bhajeta śṛvaṇādibhyo yadvidyāto vimucyate.

—Tattvadīpanibaṅdha, v.53

Bhaktimārgaḥ sarvebhyo'tiricyate

—Subodhinī, 10-68-10

The incompetence of knowledge in guiding a person on the right path was duly exposed by Duryodhana when he declared "I know what is religion, but cannot follow it; I know what is irreligion, but cannot avoid it." The path of knowledge demands an eradication of human instincts which is a difficult thing to achieve for an average man. The Bhagavadgītā has given due consideration to this aspect of human difficulty and has rightly conceded that it (this path) is too hard for those persons whose minds cannot be fixed on the Absolute. (XII·5). Tulasīdāsā, a noted poet-thinker of Hindi has similarly declared that the path of knowledge is as difficult to pursue as walking on the edge of a sword.

The path of knowledge does not suit human psychology too. According to psychology, a man's mind is a complex of cognitive, affective and conative tendencies. And if we try to determine which of these tendencies is dominant, we shall have to accept that affective or feeling tendency is easily most assertive. The path of knowledge leaves little room for this very tendency when it emphasises the sole importance of knowing the formless Supreme. Even logically it is not possible to know the Formless Unknowable without the instrumentality of something known. That is why R. Cohen and E. Nagel in their work 'An Introduction to Logic and Scientific Method' have stated "In trying to visualize the unknown, the imagination must clothe it with attributes analogous to the known." Suradasa, an illustrious poet of Hindi has exclaimed "The ways of the Absolute are unknowable."

Even Dr. Radhakrishnan has said "The Absolute . . . rigid and motionless, and totally lacking in initiative or influence cannot call forth our worship."

God has been created by man as He alone can offer him protection and security in the hour of anguish and helplessness. As Radhakrishnan puts it, human mind has a craving for "the living sense of companionship . . . in their difficult times" or supreme protector. A deep faith in such a Protector or Father gives solace and satisfaction to an individual heart lost in darkness and despair. Nay, this faith gives a society too a sense of courage and bravery to fight against injustice and oppression. Faith in God is not only good for an individual life, it is equally good for the life of a society, because like individuals societies too have to face obstacles, wage struggles, and pass through hours of hardship. "Theism has implicit in it the social hope" even according to Radhakrishnan.

Bhakti or devotion does ample justice to human psychological demand and social necessity. And what is still more important, it democratises knowledge. It makes the essence of knowledge so diluted that it can be grasped even by human beings of average mental calibre.

Vivekananda has explicitly stated "Bhakti has to float on smoothly with the currents of our nature." Indian thinkers were alive to the difficulty of the path of devotion right from beginning of their civilization. That is why it was declared that one can realize God even through sincere devotion and surrender of one's acts to Him. Patanjali who has founded a school of rigid discipline for realizing the supreme end of human life has conceded that salvation can be had even through dedication to the Lord.

We should also realize this fact that devotion is not against the path of knowledge. The paths of devotion and knowledge begin from separate streams, but that ultimately unite in the realization of the ocean of God or supreme knowledge or salvation. Beginnings are bound to be different, but what is material is their ultimate fate. That is why Vivekananda has given his clear opinion "There is not really so much difference between knowledge (jnana) and love (Bhakti) as people sometimes imagine."

The best way to judge the close relation between knowledge and devotion is to see the conduct and works of prominent persons who are famous for their philosophical systems or philosophical acumen. We should not forget that man is a total person in the sense that we find in his being emotions, thought action and everything else of the kind. It is a false concept of man which divides him into a person of knowledge or a person of sentiments and emotions. True, that in a person sometimes the urge to indulge into abstract thinking may assert self, or the urge to feel may rise like the waves of an ocean. But all these are just the ripples of his life. Rigid classification of men into men of knowledge or men of feeling and emotion is both deceptive and false.

If a person is supposed to be a man of knowledge alone, then it will imply that he is shorn of every emotion. Similarly, if a person is supposed to be a man of emotion alone, it will mean that he lacks knowledge totally. It will be like saying that if a person has heart, he has no eyes, and if he has eyes he has no heart. On the face of it, such a statement is absurd.

In the history of mankind, we therefore find persons who were accepted as the great lovers and preachers of knowledge, exhibiting great warmth of devotion, and the persons accepted as men of devotion, writing like men of knowledge to substantiate positions. Thus Narada, a man of devotion wrote 'Narada Bhakti Sutras' and the great system builders of Indian philosophy like Śaṁkara, Ramanuja, Vallabha, Madhva etc. wrote Bhakti stotras. I shall like to give a lengthier account of their devotional works.

We may begin our account from Śaṁkara, the foremost Advaita thinkar. Śaṁkara, a very great scholar, was very much aware of the fact that the unqualified Brahman, lacking name and form, cannot appeal to a great bulk of people.

And therefore for the meditation the unqualified and attributeless Brahman is given a concrete form, and thus the Nirguṇa Brahman becomes Saguṇa Brahman. This Saguṇa Brahman too can be portrayed as Rāma, Krishna, Saṁkara,

Ganeśa, or Brahmā, Viṣṇu, and Maheśa etc. In the form of an avatāra, the Supreme tries to go to the fathest extent to make people Truth-minded or what is the same thing, God-minded.

Śaṁkara's lofty Advaita becacuse of of its most generous attitude can accommodate practically all the varieties of God-worship. It cannot have any real quarrel with other shades of philosophical or religious thinking.

In keeping with the Indian tradition, Śaṁkara too accepts the adhikārībheda. Philosophy, no doubt, cannot afford to compromise on the fundamental truth, but it should certainly stoop to cater to the requirements of the individuals making effort to march in the direction of truth in their own way. If philosophy refuses to make this concession, the doors for human emancipation are closed, and philosophy shall become a privilege of a few spiritual aristocrats. The true philosopher, faithful to the spirit of real philosophy is not afraid of making concessions with a view to lead to lowly and the uninitiated to the path of light and lusture. If it is a 'sin', the true philosopher does not mind sinning. Appaya Diksita very explicitly confesses this sinning : "O Lord, I have in my weakness committed three sins and I beg forgiveness of you. To serve as a support for meditation I have tried to give a form to the Highest who is really formless: I have tried to define the indefinable by composing panegyrics litanies and lastly I have confined the omnipresent Lord to particular places of worship and have journied to those places."

Śaṁkara has observed in the introduction to the Eighth chapter of the Chandogya Upanishad : "The absolutely true Brahman, being one without a second, is regarded by persons of dull intellect as non-existent; hence what the Śruti thinks is that these persons be brought on to the right path. We shall gradually lead them up to the knowledge of the absolutely true also."

Śaṁkara is aware of human psychology. He fully understands that human beings can be weaned from a worldly attitude only by and by through a devotion to the God, who, in the words of A.N. Whitehead, must be sufficiently akin to be understood, sufficiently different to provoke attention and sufficiently great to command admiration." Śaṁkara, therefore, brings about a picture of extreme beauty. He draws the picture of Śrīkṛṣṇa who is more beautiful than the lacs of kandarpa, the god of beauty.

Even idol worship is permitted. The idol is not free from God who is all-pervading. The idol is meaningless for a person who has no faith in it. But for a person who sees the Supreme in it, it is a vehicle of supreme significance. He sees in Śala-grama not a piece of stone, but Viṣṇu, the all-pervading God. In this context the words of a modern thinker vis. Aldous Huxley may be quoted to impress the great import of an idol on the minds of ultra-modern individuals.

"The longings, emotions and imaginations of those who kneel, and for generations have knelt, before the shrine," writes Aldous Huxley, "create, as it were, an enduring vortex in the psychic medium so that the image lives with a secondary, inferior divine life projected on it by the worshippers as well as with the primary divine life which, in common with all other animate and inanimate beings, possesses in virtue of its relation to the divine gournd." Who can deny that psychologically the idol arouses the thought of the Supreme in the mind of the worshipper due to the law of association ? Those who condemn idol worship fail to understand its secret philosophy. Of course, a worshipper must not encage God only in the idol. He must proceed further. But an idol can certainly be a help to a beginner. Unnecessary criticism of idol worship is, therefore, unwarranted.

Bhakti defined

Śaṁkara gives importance to the realization of the Supreme Truth and tries to define bhakti as an instrument of achieving this objective. He clearly writes that devotion is a foremost medium of achieving liberation. Devotion consists in realizing one's true nature. And construed in this sense, bhakti becomes almost nondistinct from a curiosity of knowing the truth.

In fact devotion should be an instrument of truth realisation. This objective, placed before devotion is essential to avoid the blind alleys of fanaticism. Devotion seeks to walk in the domain of serach for truth with the aid of faith (śradhā). The latter has been defined by Śaṁkara as delimitation of our tendency for truth by the scriptures and the preceptor's preachings so that the objective can be achieved. Yes, in our bhakti we are guided by our faith in the scriptures and preachers; but the objective remains the same viz. the realization of the supreme truth that there is no difference between the jīva and Brahman.

Though Śaṁkara was a great logician and debator and shows a rare capacity of arguing in the most subtle manner, he did realize that without devotion one cannot go very far. He acknowledges that mind can be cleansed very effectively and successfully through devotion alone.

Śaṁkara did not show any tendency of calling Saguṇa Brahman as inferior to Nirguṇa Brahman though the latter is the real form of the Absolute. On the other hand he states that both are one. He goes, still further, to add that Śrīkṛṣṇa is the Supreme. He even tries to meditate on Kṛṣṇa who is standing in the forests of Vṛndāvana by the side of the Yamunā river, who is as dark as the sky and is filling the universe with His lusture, who is putttng on yellow cloth and has applied sandal wood and 'Karpura' on all His limbs, whose eyes are stretching up to ears, and who is putting on 'Kuṇḍala' in His ears, whose lotus like face is beaming with smile, who is wearing a necklace of Kaustubha maṇi, so on and so forth. In his famous composition the Mohamugdara, Śaṁkara clearly writes that the only worthy object of meditation is Viṣṇu or Kṛṣṇa.

Śaṁkara rises to the highest height of bhakti when he states "Lord, though it is true that there is no difference between you and myself, but I belong to you and you do not belong to me just as the ripple belongs to the sea and the sea never belongs to the ripple." And finally when he declares: "O Lord, whatever I do that all is your worship."

In the Praśnottara-ratna-mālikā Śaṁkara puts a query: "What is to be remembered day and night?" and he himself answers: "The feat of God and not the world." "Who are blind, even though they have eyes?" "The men not believing in scriptures and God." "What is difficult to get?" "The devotion for Hari." "By which process a man can attain liberation?" "By cultivating devotion of Mukunda." "Who is to be worshipped?" "The avatāras of God."

In the Harimīde Stotra Śaṁkara clearly states that he praises with devotion Viṣṇu, the infinite. He also makes this clear that what is subtle and beyond the range of logic can be grasped through devotion. In the Vedanta Stotrāni again he repeats that the Supreme can be known through faith, devotion, meditation etc. The famous Acyutāṣṭakaṁ states that the Lord becomes submissive to a man who recites that panegyric. In the commentary on the Viṣṇu-sahasranāma, Śaṁkara expressly states that Kṛṣṇa is the Supreme, the Truth, consciousness or knowledge, and bliss.

Answering to a query whether abandoning of scriptural acts and merely following the path of knowledge can lead the house-holders to liberation, Śaṁkara writes in his commentary on the Bhagavadgītā that the latter aims at a combination of Jñāna and karma, knowledge and action. This implies, since devotion is just a combination of knowledge and action that it is appreciated even by Śaṁkara. Śaṁkara even preaches the gospel of doing actions to please God.

Śaṁkara suggests that only those actions are to be avoided which tend to turn human beings in undesirable directions. He approves this point of view that any person reposing complete faith in God becomes liberated. He accepts quite willingly the position that a person who develops firm devotion for the Supreme at the time of his departure from this world attains the Supreme. He never doubts that whatever is offered by a man of devotion to the Supreme is accepted by Him. By cultivating an attachment for God, by worshipping Him, by becoming his devotee a person attains the Selfhood, the highest stage reached by the path of knowledge too. Śaṁkara leaves no doubt that by a sincere devotion, God can be known in His original and real form. He even clearly accepts the position that the people of sincere devotion are the best. The devotees are persons most dear to the Supreme.

The devotees, therefore, can certainly attain the highest state of liberation. Nothing that is devoid of faith can be efficacious. Be it a penance, or an act of alms giving or anything else like knowledge.

Śaṁkara has not tried to hide that even a man of knowledge is able to know the real nature of Brahman only when he is endowed with devotion. The purport of the whole process of a search of the Supreme is that a person can attain the highest stage only by a spirit of complete dedication to the Supreme. And thus we come to the conclusion that even according to Śaṁkara the path of devotion is that road which leads a man to the highest stage, his ultimate objective, in an unerring way and an unfaltering manner.

The fact is that Śaṁkara never underestimated the value of faith and devotion. Even in his Nirguṇa Mānasa Pūjā he tries to worship the self with the water of the river of faith to attain the state of ultimate liberation.

Śaṁkara, of course, held no brief for a sentimental and shallow bhakti. If a devotee thinks that ultimately he and the object of his devotion are distinct and different, he is wrong. The real devotion leads a man from "unreality to reality, from darkness to light, from death to immortality." This very thought led Śaṁkara to distinguish between two kinds of devotion.

Two kinds of bhakti

Śaṁkara states in his Prabodha Sudhākara that there are two kinds of bhakti, one subtle and the other gross. The gross bhakti comes in the beginning and later on subtle from of bhakti appears. He is right.

In the initial stages a person is drawn towards God by some mundane desire. He wants peace of mind; or seeks riches, or desires fulfilment of some desire or something else of the kind. By and by, a man rises higher and higher in the rungs of subtle bhakti where from a mere worship a person develops a state of dedication ultimately leading to the purging of mind from all sensual thoughts. Thus from the state of unreality he rises to the state of reality, from darkness he comes to light.

Itis desirable and in the fitness of things that a man should continue his march towards the highest stage of bhakti. But even in the lower stage, bhakti is not worth condemnation.

The rituals and ceremonial offerings have their own influence on the minds of the devotees. Due to faith a mysterious 'aura' is build around God present before the devotees in the form of idols and statues and a deeper meaning of life is awakened in their hearts. The deovtees, even in their initial stages, transcend the limitations of a sheer mundane and material life. The seeds of a spiritual attitude is thus laid in the human hearts which grow in the form of trees in the days to come. The Chāndogya Upanishad makes a point to note this fact. Therefore it states that it is all the better if one understands and grasps the meaning and significance of the mantras that he recites, but even if one does not understand the meaning of the mantras, it will do him only good to recite them with faith. Śaṁkara thus does not condemn devotion at any stage. Only he would insist on the fuller understanding of the import of a symbol to enable a man in the direction of rising to the highest level.

We can safely conclude, therefore, that Śaṁkara does not refuse to give due recognition to devotion for, as some men are of inferior, others middling, other again of superior intelligence, not all are capable of fixing their mind on the infinite Brahman devoid of any change or transformation."

Perhaps the philosophy of Śaṁkara devotion is summarised by Sri Ramakrishṇa in the following words :

"Brahman may be compared to an infinite ocean, without beginning or end. Just as, through intense cold, some portions of the ocean freeze into ice and the formless water appears to have form, so through the intense love of the devotee Brahman appears to take on form and personality. But the form melts away again as the sun of knowledge rises. Then the universe also disappears, and there is seen to be nothing but Brahman, the infinite."

We may now proceed to consider the views of Rāmānuja, another noted Vedanti thinker. He held the view that man has a real soul. The conscious and the unconscious are dependent on the Supreme as boby is dependent on the soul. The bondage of the soul to the body has to be destroyed, because the latter delimits soul's consciousness. This bondage can be best destroyed through the grace of God. The best ideal of human life is kainkarya or living in the service of the Lord. Unless God's blessings descend on the self, the latter's story of agonies cannot come to an end.

In this context the following words of Rāmānuja are significant:

"We know from scriptures that there is Supreme Person whose nature is absolute bliss and goodness; who is fundamentally antagonistic to all evil: who is the cause of the origination and sustentation and dissolution of the world; who differs in nature from all other beings; who is all knowling, who by his mere thought and will accomplishes all the purposes: who is an ocean of kindness as it were, for all who depend on him who is all-merciful; who is immeeasurably raised above all possibility of any one being equal or superior to him; whose name is the highest Brahman. And with equal certainty we know from scriptures that this Supreme Lord, when pleased by the faithful worship of his devotees—which worship consists in daily repeated meditation on Him, assisted by the performance of all the practices proseribed for each caste and aśrama frees them from the influence of nescience which consists of karma accumulated in the infinite progress of time and hence hard to overcome, allows them to attain to that supreme bliss which consists in the direct intuition of his own true nature; and after that does not turn them back into the miseries of Saṁsāra. . . . As moreover, the released soul has freed itself from the bondage of Karma, has its powers of knowledge fully developed and has all its being, in the supremely blissful intuition of the highest Brahman, it evidently cannot desire anything else, nor enter on any other form of activity and the idea of its returning into the Saṁsāra, therefore, is altogether excluded. Nor indeed need we fear that the Supreme Lord when once having taken to himself the devotee whom He greatly loves, will turn him back into the Saṁsāra. . . ."

Rāmānuja prefers to understand by bhakti what he himself calls steady remembrance. He writes, steady remembrance of this kind is designated by the word 'devotion' (bhakti): for this term has the same meaning as upāsanā (meditation). For this reason scripture and smṛti agree in making the following declarations: 'A man knowing him possesses death' (Svet. Up.

III. 8): 'knowing thus the man becomes immortal.' (Tai. Up. III.12. 7), 'Neither by the Vedas nor by gifts, nor by austerities, nor by sacrifice can I be so seen as thou hast seen me. But by devotion I may in this form be known and seen in truth, O Arjuna, and also be entered into. (Bh. Gi. XI-53, 54): That highest Person O Partha, may be obtained by exclusive devotion.' (VIII, 22)

Rāmānuja distinguishes between two kinds of knowledge. There is knowledge which springs from the study of the scriptures and there is another variety of knowledge that is born out of concentrated meditation. The latter kind of knowledge is higher and is also known as Upāsanā. It is by nature a devout meditation (bhakti) and consists in direct intuition of Brahman.

We clearly find in Rāmānuja a tendency of synthesizing the elements of jñāna, karma, and bhakti i.e. knowledge, action and devotion. This is a very healthy attitude towards meditation of the Supreme. Psychologically, knowledge gained by a study of the scriptures makes a man lean Supreme and cultivate an attitude of detachment towards the mundane objects. The actions consecrated by the desire of pleasing the Supreme do impress the mind of a person in the right direction. And thus a situation is created which helps a person develop a real devotion for the Lord. The devotion which thus proceeds to "know, and see and gain the Lord in His real nature" becomes a great asset in the task of God realization. Rāmānuja has tried to state the characteristics of true bhaktas, devotees.

"Firstly, the Bhakta's only happiness consists in being with God, and his misery in being without God; secondly the Bhakta attributes all his afflictions to his own guilt; thirdly, the bhakta has implicit belief that all beings are sbject to God's sovereign rule. Hence, the Bhakta is free from every trace of enmity. He who possesses these qualifications come to me. This coming into Me implies realizing me as I am in reality i.e. resting in blessed enjoyment of the Divine that is devoid of the faintest trace of anything like the defects of nescience."

Similarly, on another occasion, Rāmānuja tries to portray the conduct of a devout devotee. "Thus, then in conclusion thou shalt carry on all thy worldly duties required for thy bodily subsistence and scriptural duties viz. daily, casual etc. rites in order to please Me, (God) as done by one who is essentially my liege, and actuated to do, by myself, Thou shalt ever in love be engaged in lovingly singing My praises, in My service, in bowing, etc. Thou shalt contemplate that the universe is under My rule and guidance, and subsist as essentially My appendage. Thou shalt ponder and reflect over the multitude of My lovable attributes. Occupying thyself daily, thus, in devotion of the aforesaid description thou shalt reach Myself."

It should not be understood that anybody can love the Supreme in any mental condition. An attachment to the supreme becomes possible only when the mind is freed from the traces of sins and nescience. "It is only to one who is entirely cleansed of all his sins that I became the object of love. It is only such a person who would converge all the strength of his intellect to me as his sole aim."

The right type of devotion leads a person finally to a cultivation of a tendency of absolute self-surrender, which has been termed prapatti by Rāmānuja. It has also been described as śaraṇāgati. In fact, he wrote a beautiful prose-poem called śaraṇāgati Gadya in which we find the highest spirit of self-surrender expressed.

Like Arjuna who surrendered his own self to the supreme, Rāmānuja surrenders his self to the Supreme. Just as this dedication on the part of Arjuna gives him the necessary trust in the supreme and endows him with a spirit of rare confidence, and lifts him to attitude of complete trust and confidence in the Supreme. Perhaps, Rāmānuja was inspired to write about this spirit of complete dedication by the famous verse of the Bhagavadagītā viz. "Surrendering all duties to Me, seek refuge in me alone, I shall absolve you of all sins; grieve not. The devout heart of Rāmānuja took a special note of the word' śaraṇa' occurring there. He must have noted that when one has sought the shelter of the Supreme, there is no need of any religious dectrine (sarva dharmāna parityajya). When cnce an individual has resigned himself to God, nothing further is needed.

There should be no surprise, therefore, when we find that Rāmānuja declares that he seeks the refuge of the Supreme shelter. He addresses the lord as parabrahmabhūta, and as the great ocean of unlimited kindness, gentleness, parental affection, bountifulness, majesty, and beauty. He says that leaving all other things, he seeks the shelter of the Lord. And finally the last word in dedication is declared when he writes: "My Lord, you alone are my mother, you alone are my father, you alone are my brother, you alone are my friend, you alone are learning, you alone are the riches, you alone are my all."

The Yatindramata Dīpikā, which can be considered as an introduction to Rāmānuja's philosophy, has brought out the characteristic features of a dedicated person (prapanna) in the following words:

"The prapanna is one who has resorted to God and alone, being helpless and devoid of any other refuge. He is also of two kinds, one who seeks the three ends of life (Dharma, Artha and Kama) and the other who seeks final liberation (Mokṣa). The one who seeks final liberation learns from the company of good souls to distinguish between what is eternal and what is non-eternal. This engenders in him a spirit of datachment from things worldly which will lead to the desire of detachment from the world, i.e. liberation. He then resorts to a teacher who possesses the excellences of a good preceptor, who leads him to Śrī, the Lady of Mercy who acts as the mediator between him and the Lord. His only means for liberation are the holy feet of Nārāyaṇa. This way to the Lord is open to all in the world despite caste or creed."

The way of the ārta prapanna is of different type and mould. "The ārta prapanna is one who after accepting prapatti as the means continues to perform all nitya and naimittika duties as ends in themselves on account of their being consecrated to the Lord. He avoids doing anything which would offend the Lord and His devotees." Rāmānuja was a philosopher of supreme theistic attitude. He has always tried to equate the object of human worship with the Great Supreme. In fact, he believed in the Divine Personality as is brought out lucidly in his commentary on one of the Sūtras of the Brahma Sūtras. He writes :

". . . .The form of this person (in the eye) is the same as that person yonder (in the sun), the joints of the one is the joints of the other, the name of the one is the name of the other."

"The person who is perceived within the sun and within the eye, is something different from the individual soul, viz. the highest soul ; because there are declared qualities belonging to that. The text ascribes to him the quality of having risen above, i.e. being free from all evil and this can belong to the highest self only, not to the individual soul. For to be free from all evil means to be free from the influence of karma, and this quality can belong to the highest self only differing from all individual souls which, as is shown by their experience of pleasure and pain are in the bonds of Karma. Those essential qualities also which presuppose freedom from all evil such as mastery over all worlds and wishes, capability of realizing one's purposes, being the inner self of all, etc. belong to the highest Self alone."

Vallabhacarya, yet another ācārya who founded a distinct school of the Advaita gave utmost importance to devotion. His philosophical system has been called the Suddhadvaita. It is also known as the path of grace (Puśti Mārga). Vallabha was of this view that liberation can be realised only through divine grace. Unless one makes a complete surrender to God through love, one cannot attain salvation. But a true devotee does not like liberation. He wants to live in the ever persent proximity of God.

Vallabha held four authorities in high esteem viz. the Vedas, the Brahmasūtras, the Bhagavadgītā and the Bhāgavata Puraṇa. He defined Bhakti as the firm and overwhelming love for the Lord coupled with a full sense of His greatness. It is not the view that knowledge is useless. The only point that is stressed is that even knowledge if it is not associated with devotion, cannot help us in realizing our aim of spiritual height. It is possible to destroy Maya only through devotion, because in devotion ego is destroyed, while in knowledge it may not be completely annihilated.

Path of Puśti or God's grace is open to every person irrespective of caste or creed or sex. Our biggest endeavour should be to cultivate devotion of the Lord Kṛṣṇa.

Śrīkṛṣṇa is the God worshipped by the Bhāgavata. He was the real hero of the Mahābhārata. He had given the sermon known as the Bhagavadgītā. Thus for Vallabha Śrīkṛṣṇa is not a person. He is God himself. There is no other God. Therefore the very first thing preached by the Puṣṭi Marga is to seek the protection of Śrikṛṣṇa. Every person must proclaim "Sṛikrsna is my shelter". Naturally therefore one must try to effect a complete, unstinted self-surrender to the Lord. Everything—body, senses, vital breaths, inner organ and the soul—are surrendered.

Ordinarily the term 'puṣṭi' means the strength of the body. The Puṣṭi Mārga, if interpreted in this manner, shall become a doctrine of 'eat, drink, and be merry'. But Vallabha does not mean strength of the body by the term. He has derived the word from the Bhāgavata which takes it in the sense of favour of God. Vallabha has drawn heavily from the Bhāgavata in interpreting his doctrine of Puṣṭi. The Bhāgavata states that the Supreme is like the Kalpa tree that yields the desire desired by any one under it. He gives the desired things to a desirous devotee. He gives the desirable things even to a devotee who does not desire anything. Similary, the Bhāgavata establishes the importance of a selfless devotion. God's favour can be obtained only through this method. The sole aim of this devotion is a complete self-surrender. The factor of God's shelter is a predominant note of the Bhāgavata. To seek the shelter of any one else than Śrīkṛṣṇa has been described a foolish act like that of attempting to cross the ocean by grasping the tail of a foolish dog.

In his work Navaratnam Vallabha has tried to show that the principle of self-surrender should be the dominant note of a devotee's life. He should not have any worry whatsoever. God is omnipotent. Why should one worry then when he has surrendered himself completely at His feet? Let him only repeat "Śrīkṛṣṇa is my refuge".

In his work Antaḥkaraṇa Prabodha, Vallabha has reiterated that there is no God other than Kṛṣṇa. The best way to be happy lies in dedication and devotion and performing our duties as servants of the Supreme. If we do our duty, the Lord shall definitely do his.

Vallabha's another work Vivekadhairyaśraynirupaṅaṁ persuades an individual to bear with grace all the three kinds of pain which are either adhibhautika, adhyātmika, or adhidaivika in nature. Let him not forget that Hari is capable of doing everything. He can make possible, what is otherwise impossible and vice versa.

Bhaktivardhinī, Vallabha's other work, tries to show how the devotion for God can be inculcated and developed. Ordinarily, the seeds of devotion are born in human mind only due to the favour of God. By and by, this seed grows in the form of a tree of devotion by means of listening to God's glory, and renunciation of the attachment for the worldly objects. And when finally this devotion becomes deep-rooted in human mind the individual becomes a blessed soul. His life becomes successful.

The Sevāphala, another work of Vallabha, points out six things resulting from service to God. The first thing is the Alaukika Sāmārthya or unasual capacity. A person experiences in it the undescribable blissful experience of the Divine. The second thing is Sayujya, which signifies in the sense in which it is interpreted by the followers of Puṣṭi Mārga, a sense of equality like that of the cowherd boys who played with Śrīkṛṣṇa. According to others, it means the experience of communion with the Supreme. The third thing is Sevopayogī Deha or obtaining a body which is capable of doing service to God in Vaikuṇṭha or Gokula, Vṛndāvana etc. It may mean then becoming a creeper, bird, animal etc. in the place where Śrīkṛṣṇa appeared. The fourth thing is Udvega or mental disquiteness. Mind becomes unstable because of sin or fear. This should be checked. The fifth thing is attachment to the traditional behaviour. It has been called 'Pratibandha'. And final outcome is Bhoga or a tendency to enjoy. To desire worldly things of enjoyment is bad. But if one desires to enjoy the supernatural grace and the favour of the Supreme it is desirable.

The Madhurāṣtaka of Vallabha is a specimen of his intense devotion for Śrīkṛṣṇa, It records the fact how every limb, every act, every part, every behaivour of Śrīkṛṣṇa is graceful and enchanting. The whole panegeric is a fine example of the mental tendency generated in the mind of devotee when he cultivates a deep-rooted and whole-hearted affection for Śrīkṛṣṇa. Vallabha finally summarizes his emotion by writing "Everything belonging to the Lord of lusciousness and sweetness is captivating."

Vallabha has distinguished between three ways of God realization. By an inculcation of jñāna, knowledge, a person becomes learned in everything; by following the path of action and rituals, his mind is pleased. But by pursuing the holy path of bhakti, devotion, Śrīkṛṣṇa the Supreme, is pleased. But for Vallabha the path of devotion is the only path worth pursuing. Hence, he advises everybody to devote oneself completely to Hari, leaving everything else apart, through listening etc.

Vallabha has openly and clearly indicated his preference for the path of devotion by stating that the path of knowlwedge may lead to confusion, and therefore the only safe path is the devotion of Śrīkṛṣṇa. The devotees are always very pure; in fact there is none who can be termed purer than a devotee.

Vallabha has distinguished between two kinds of bhakti. One is called Maryādā Bhakti and the other has been termed Puṣṭi Bhakti. The devotion of the feet of the Supreme has been called Maryādā Bhakti; while the devotion of the face of God has been known as 'Puṣṭi Bhakti'. In the former a desire for some result and reward is present; in the latter there is no desire for such a reward. The former leads to the liberation called Sāyujya, i.e. identification with God, while the latter leads to a sense of nondistinction between one thing and the other, all things being just God hidden.

One thing more is to be noted. Vallabha has described the path of devotion advocated my him as "nirguṇa" bhakti yoga. As in other cases, in the case of this description of devotion, Vallabha has drawn inspiration from the Bhāgavata. The Bhāgavata has described this 'nirguṇa' bhakti as a tendency of an intense and spontaneous flow of attachment to god, unhindered by any worldly obstruction, like the mighty current of Ganges defying the obstructions of the mountains and stones and flowing towards the ocean. Once this type of devotion is developed, it becomes deeply rooted in mind and, therefore, lasts for ever. As is evident, this type of devotion is free from any trace of desire or wish for reward. Vallabha also means this very kind of devotion. A service of Śrīkṛṣṇa without any trace of desire is what Vallabha commends. This type of devotion results in a blissful state generated from the state of mind thus cultivated. For such a devotee even the liberation of various kinds have no temptations. Vallabha has recommended this very selfless, spontaneous devotion in his Chatuḥ Ślokī. A seeker of 'nirguṇa' bhakti has specific frame of mind untainted by worldly desires and mundane ambitions. His religion is the service of Śrīkṛṣṇa, his wish is to see Him, and his liberation consistent and unperturbed service and devotion of Śrikṛṣṇa.

We have many persons of knowledge who gave due importance to devotion. We can consider Kabira as a prominent thinker of the Advaita thought. For him the Reality is by nature such that it has neither head, nor form. It is thinner than the scent of a flower.

(Jāke muha māthā nahī, nāhī rūpaka rūpa
puhupa basa thai pātalā, aisā tatta anūpa)

It is something that defies description. But its brilliance is more bright than the light of hundreds of the suns lying in one line.

(pārabrahma ke teja kā kaisā hai unamāna

Kahibe kūṅ sobhā nahī, dekhyāñ ī paravāna.

Kabīra teja ananta kā, mānau ūgī sūraja seṇi
pati saṅga jāgī sundarī, kautiga dīṭhā teṇī.)

Despite this unique nature of Reality, Kabīra considers it to be an object of devotion. He calls it Rāma and considers Him omnipotent.

(Sāī sūṅ saba hota hai, bande thai kuchha nāhī
rāī thai parabata karai, parabata rāī māhiṅ)

He is of this firm opinion that this Supreme can be realized only through devotion. A person who does not cultivate such a devotion wastes his entire life.

(jihi ghata priti na prema rasa, puni rasanā nahi rāma
te nara isa saṅsāra me, upaji khaye bekāma.)

He believes in a complete surrender to the Supreme out of Love.Let a person become a dog driven by his master.

(kabīra kutā rāma kā, motiyā merā nāu
rāma nāma kī jevadī jita khaichai tita jāu)

A person should be so attached to the Lord, that every moment he should feel restless in His absence.

(kabīra dekhata dina gayā, nisi bhi dekhata jāi
birahaṇī piba pāvai nahī, jiyarā talapai māi)

Kabīra considers himself to be a bride of the Lord and loves Him with a rare intensity.

(hari morā pīva, mai rāma ki bahuriā
rāma baḍe mai chhutaka lahuriā)

Unless the ego is completely destroyed through such an intense devotion one cannot attain the Lord.

(sati sūrā tana sāhi kari tana mana kiya ghāṇa
diyā mahaulā pīva kūṅ taba madahata karai bakhāṇa)

But Kabīra never forgets that the supreme is the sole reality. Everything has emanated from Him.

(eka būṅda ekai mala mūtara eka charma eka gūdā
eka jyoti thai saba utapannā ko brahmana, ko sūdā)

Hence, Kabīra always preached that the best way of realizing the Lord is devotion, a selfless devotion.

(kabira kahatā jāta hai, sunatā hai saba koya
rāma kahe bhalā hoiga, nahi tara bhalā na hoya)

Another thinker who deserves our attention because of his prominent emphasis on devotion is Tulasīdāsa, who was well-versed in the Advaitic teaching. He is aware of the fact that real knowledge consists in seeing the Supreme in everything (dekha brahma samāna saba māhi), there is no multiplicity in the universe from the stand-point of ultimate truth (so tāi tohi nahi bheda i.e. neha nānāsti kiṅchana); ultimately there is no distinction between the self and the Supreme (sohamasmi iti vritti akhaṇdā) and the ultimate bliss consists in experiencing the Supreme or the Brahman (brahma sukhahi anubhavahi anūpā akatha anāmaya nāma na rūpā.)

But Tulasīdāsa is aware of the fact that the path of knowledge is very tough. It is just like walking on the edge of a sword.

(gyāna pantha kripāna kai dhārā
parata khagesa hoi nahi bārā. and
gyāna agama pratyūha anekā
sādhana kaṭḥina na mana kahu tekā.)

But devotion is very easy to cultivate. Therefore, wise persons try to cultivate devotion for God rather than running after the tough path of knowledge.

(asa vichāri hari bhagata sayāne
mukuti nirādari bhagati lobhāne. and
śruti purāna saba grantha kahahī
Raghupati bhagati binā sukha nahī. and
rāma bhagati chintāmani sūndara, or
raghupati bhagati sajivani mūri.)

According to Tulasidāsa, there is no difference in devotion and knowledge from the standpoint of ultimate attainment. Both free man's mind from the various attachments.

(bhagatihi gyānahi nahi kachhu bhedā
ubhaya harahi bhava sambhava khedā. and
mana te sakala vāsanā bhāgi
Kevala rāma charana laya lāgi.)

Tulasidāsa has clearly stated that without devotion liberation cannot be attained. Thus even our highest aim of life needs the cultivation of devotion for the Lord.

(binu hari bhajana na bhava tariya.
yaha siddhānta apela.)

Swami Vivekanada was a great Vedānti thinker and said in his poem 'The Song of the Sanyasin'

"Wake up the note, the song that had its birth
Far off, where worldly taint could never reach,
In mountain caves, and glades of forest deep,
Whose calm no sigh for lust or wealth or fame
Could ever dare to break; where rolled the stream
Of knowledge, truth, and bliss that follows both.
Sing high that note, Sanyasin bold. Say
'Om Tat Sat, Om.'

Let darkness go, the will-o' -the wisp that leads
With blinking light to pile more gloom on gloom
This thirst for life, for ever quench; it drags
From birth to death, and death to birth, the soul.
He conquers all who conquers self. Know this
And never yield, Sanyasi bold. Say—
'Om Tat Sat, Om.'

They know not truth who dream such vacant dreams
As father, mother, children, wife and friend.
The sexless Self, whose father He ? whose child ?
Whose friend, whose foe is He who is but One ?
The Self is all in all, none else exists;
And thou art That, Sanyasin, bold. Say-
'Om Tat Sat, Om.'

There is but One-The Free- The Knower- Self.
Without a name, without a form or stain.
In Him is Maya, dreaming all this dream.
The Witness, He appears as nature, soul.
Know thou art That, Sanyasin bold. Say-
'Om Tat Sat, Om.'

Thus day by day, till Karma's powers spent
Release the soul for ever. No more is birth.
Nor I, nor thou, nor God, nor man. The 'I'
Has All become, the All is 'I' and Bliss.
Know thou art That, Sanyasin bold. Say-
'Om Tat Sat, Om.'

The above song makes it clear that Vivekananda believed in Śaṅkara's Advaitic philosophy that the Brahman alone is real and world is merely an empirical reality. But even he believed in the efficacy of Bhakti-yoga. He said, "The personal God is the highest possible reading of the Absolute by the human mind" (Complete Works of Vivekananda, vol. III, p. 37) and declares "Bhakti Yoga is a real, genuine search after the Lord, a search beginning, continuing, ending in Love. One single moment of the madness of extreme love of God brings us eternal freedom." (Ibid, p. 31).

Shri Ramakrishna Paramahamsa, Vivekananda's Master, was a great Jnānin, a liberated soul (Paramahaṁsa). But For most of his disciples he recommended Bhakti yoga.

because the path of devotion is a natural one leading to realization. Everyone has love in his heart—it merely needs to be directed toward God ; and for a follower of bhakti yoga discrimination, dispassion, and all the other virtues unfold easily and naturally." Shri Ramakrishna used to preach 'The more you move toward the light, the farther you will be from darkness.'

Shri Ramakrishna himsalf used to pray to Goddess Durgā, "O Mother, here is sin and here is virtue ; take them both and grant me pure love for thee. Here is knowledge and here is ignorance ; I lay them at thy feet. Grant me pure love for thee. Here is purity and here is impurity ; take them both and grant me pure love for thee. Here are good works and here are evil works ; I lay them at thy feet. Grant me pure love for thee." (Kathāmṛta, vol. I, p. 54) He used to preach to his disciples:

"Wash away all the impurities of your mind ; then let the Lord be seated within the lotus of your heart. Meditate on him as living presence. Tie your mind to the feet of your Chosen Ideal with a silken thread, but remember not merely to think of him while you are formally meditating ; keep recollectedness at other times. Don't you know that in the shrine of Mother Durgā a light burns continually before the image, and the housewife sees to it that the light never goes out ? Keep the light of awareness always burning within your heart. Keep your thoughts awake. While engaged in your daily activities, occasionally gaze inward and see if the light is burning." (Līlāprasaṅga, Gurubhāva, Pt. I, pp. 89-90)

It is thus clear that even for perfect persons of knowledge like Ramkrishna devotion is quite necessary to attain the final mental frame that gives liberation.

Next, we may proceed to consider the views of Aurobindo. He was definitely a man of knowledge. He called his system Realistic Advaita because he did not like to dismiss this world as a mirage or illusion like Śaṁkara. He believed in the Divine Being who is beyond all relativities and defies description. It is absolute in nature because it is free to include and decide in its unique manner the forms of its expression. It is all-comprehensive and self-sustaining. Aurobindo describes its nature in his great work 'Savitri' in the following words :

"Above her little finite steps she feels
Careless of knot or pause, worlds which weave out
A strange perfection beyond law of rule,
A universe of self-found felicity,
An impressive rhythm of timeless beats,
The many-movemented heart-beats of the One,
Magic of the boundless harmonies of self,
Order of the freedom of the infinite,
The world-plastics of the Absolute
There is the All-Truth and there the timeless bliss."

He states in his The Life Divine

"The absolute manifests itself into two terms, a Being and Becoming. The Being is the fundamental reality, the Becoming is an effectual reality. It is a dynamic power and result, a creative energy and working out of the Being, a constantly persistent yet mutable form, process, outcome of its immutable formless essence." He repeats:

"It is our first premise that the Absolute is the supreme reality."

Throwing light on the unique natute of this Absolute, Aurobindo writes "it is not itself sheer emptiness for a vacant Absolute is no Absolute ; our conception of a Void or Zero is only conceptual sign of our mental inability to know or grasp it ; it bears in itself some ineffable essentiality of all that can be ; and since it holds in itself this essentiality and its possibility, it must also hold in itself in some way of its Absoluteness either the permanent truth or the inherent, even if latent, realisable actuality of all that is fundamental to our or to the world's existence."

Aurobindo conceives the Supreme as Divine Mother. The whole world is a manifestation of this Divine Mother. It is her Līlā. The mother has innumerable powers which are expressed through diverse menifestations. Though there are innumerable menifestations, four manifestations are important.

These ". . four powers of the Mother (are) (i) divine consciousness Force that dominates all existence, (ii) Transcendent, the original supreme Shakti stands above the world and links the creation to the ever unmanifest mystery of the Supreme. (iii) Universal, the Cosmic Mahashakti, she creates all these beings and contains and enters, supports and conducts all these million processes and forces. (iv) Individual." ('The Mother' by Aurobindo).

The integral Yoga of Aurobindo aims at purifying man's heart so that he may establish unity with the Divine. We must lead an inward life. The real knowledge dawns only when devotion for the Divine Mother is developed. This devotion gives ultimate knowledge of harmony with the Mother and eradicates ignorance that separates him from the Mother. Mother, as the word itself suggests, is full of love and affection for her devotees. A sense of dedication to the Mother eradicates the ego which is responsible for a sense of separateness from the infinite. Thus devotion is the gateway of liberation from worldly ignorance. Aurobindo states ; "To walk through life armoured against all fear, peril and disaster, only two things are needed, two that always go together. The grace of the Divine Mother and on your side an inner state made of faith, sincerity and surrender." (The Mother).

We can also try to learn the views of Radhakrishnan so far as devotion or Bhakti is concerned. Radhakrishnan is the best interpreter of Indian Philosophy in the modern period. He has impressed even the modern Western thinkers with his brilliance and philosophical acumen. In his famous work 'An Idealist View of Life' he has established that the ideal world alone is real and it lies beyond the phenomenal world of appearance and dominates the latter. The foundation of the universe is the transcendent, the Brahman or the Absolute.

But Radhakrishnan had enough respect for the path of devotion. Throwing light on the importance of devotion he writes : "It is often said that man is incurably religious. He must have some object or person or cause on which to fix his devotion. The instinct, if we may call it by that name, may become perverted and abused but the need is there. It must be turned to an ideal which is genuine, grounded in truth, an ideal that touches the deepest springs of man's inner life. What a man believes has a determining influence on his character."

He has given his definition of devotion. "Bhakti is conscious recognition of and whole-hearted response to the source of all goodness, the Divine. It is said 'in this world, not vows, not pilgrimages, not yoga practices, not study of scriptures, not sacrificial rites, not philosophical discourses; only devotion can give us freedom." He further adds, "Devotion implies obedience to the will of the Supreme in all our activities. It brings deliverance from anxiety about the necessities of life."

Not only Bhakti is needed for the upliftment of spiritual life. It also opens "the way to illumination". He appreciates the declaration of the Nārada Bhakti Sūtra, "When adored with love God speedily manifests himself and gives his devotees perception." Thus Radhakrishnan recognizes the importance of devotion.

We may conclude this account by acquainting ourselves with the views of Ravindranath Tagore He was a talented thinker and won even the Nobel Prize for his work 'Gitānjali'.

There is no doubt that Ravindranath was a man of devotion. For example, he sings,

"Though you are infinite, you sing in my area; that is why your light in me appears so enchanting. O One-without-form, you play in so innumerable colours, odours, songs and lyrics, and consequently the city of my heart is aroused with pleasure. When a meeting between my self and your Self takes place, the mystery is solved, and the whole universe becomes agitated with bliss. Your light has no shadow. That takes body in me and becomes enchatingly beautiful because of my tears."

(Simāra mājhe asīma tumi
bājāo āpana sura
āmāra madhye tomara prakasha
tāī eta madhura.
kata varṇe, kata gandhe,

kata gāne kata chhande-
arūpa, tomāra rūpera lilāya
jāge hrdayapura.
Tomāya āmāya milana hole
sakal jāya khule
vishva-sāgara ḍheu khelāya
uṭhe takhana ḍhule.
Tomāra aloya nāī to chhāya
āmāra mājhe pāya se kāyā,
haya se āmāra ashrujale
sundara vidhura)

On another occasion he gives expression to his feelings in the following words which portray the intensity of his devotion :

"O Hari, I, running in the forest of the world all alone, call you all the while. I cannot find my path as the darkness is deep and the water of my tears fills my eyes. I always think—'What should I do, and what I should not do; I do not know when the night of death shall descend.' I am terribly afraid and constantly recite the name 'Hari, Hari'. In the whole world, Hari alone is mine. I feel that my tears shall not be wasted. All call you the lover of devotees. This hope has encouraged me to consider you as my protector, and am saved only because of it."

(Hari, tomāya dāki, saṅsāre ekākī
āndhāra araṇye dhāi he.
gahana timire nayanera nīre
patha khunje nāhi pai he.
sadā mane haya ki karī ki karī
kakhana āsibe kāla-vibhavariī ?
tāī bhaye mari, dāki hari, hari,
hari binā keha nāī he.

nayanera jala have nā viphala,
tomāya sabe bale bhakata-vatsala.
sei āshā mane karechhi sambala,
benche āchhi shudhu tāī he.

—Gitavitāna

Let us see still another song of Ravindranath :

"Brother, what are you looking through your both the eyes fixed on my heart ? Have you pardoned me for all my errors, weaknesses, and short-comings ? Lord, how many times the days-shorn of-worship and nights-shorn of-service have come and gone, and those flowers have fallen down in the strange forests with which I should have worshipped you !"

"Kī dekhchha bandhu marama mājhāre
rākhiyā nayana duti.
karechha ki kshamā jateka āmāra
skhalana patana truti ?
pujāhīna dina-sevahina rāta
kata bāra bāra phire gechhe nātha,
arhgya kusuma jhare pare gechhe
vijana vipine lūti

—Jivana Devatā, Chitrā

The culmination of this spirit of devotion is reached in the following song of Ravindranath:

"Lord, bend my head at the bottom of the dust of thy feet, drown my entire ego in the water of these eyes. I only insult myself, when I try to bestow glory on my own self. I am dying every moment by surrounding my self through my own self. O Lord, may I not advertise myself through my acts; let thy desire be fulfilled in my life. I crave for thy absolute peace, I crave for thy absolute light. Lord, please stand in the petal of the lotus of my heart behind me."

(āmāra māthā nata kare dāo he
tomāra charana dhūlāra tale
sakala ahaṁkara he amara
dubao chokhera jale.
nijere karite gaurava-dāna
nijere kevalai kari apamāna,
āpanāre shudhū gheriyā gheriyā
ghure mare pale pale.
āmāra yena nā kari prachāra
āmāra sakala kāje,
tomāri ichchha hauka pūrṇa
āmāra jīvana mājhe.
yāchi he tomāra charama shānti
parane tomāra parama kanti
amare adala kariya dāndao
hridaya-padma-dale.)

Thus we find that even the persons of knowledge i.e. those persons who prefer to follow the path of abstruse knowledge have to acknowledge the importance of bhakti. The Garuḍa Purāṇa has rightly stated that God does not reside in the wood or stone or mud. He resides only in feeling. Hence Feeling alone is important.

(na kāṣṭhe vidyate devo na pāṣāṇe na mṛtsu ca
bhāve hi vidyate devastasmāda bhāvo hi kāraṇaṁ.)

—Garuḍa Uttara 28/11

For a person of devotion the flowers of worship are not physical or material. They are the sublime attitudes of mind. It has been rightly stated that real flowers are non-violence, self-restraint, kindness to beings, forgiveness, mental peace, meditation, knowledge and truthfulness. God is pleased when worshipped through these flowers. Other flowers are merely outside aids.

(ahiṁsā prathamaṁ puṣpaṁ dvitiyaṁ karaṇagrahaḥ
tratiyakaṁ bhūtadayā caturthaṁ kśantireva ca.
śamastu paṅcamaṁ puṣpaṁ dhyānaṁ jnānaṁ viśaṣtaḥ,
satyaṁ caivāṣṭamaṁ puṣpametaistuṣyati keṣavaḥ.
etairevaṣṭabhih puṣpaihstuṣyate cārcito hariḥ,
puṣpāntarāṇi santyeva bahyāni nṛpasattama.)

God looks inside our hearts and responds to our internal feelings. External means are just aids to stimulate those fine feelings.

6

Bhakti and Indian Culture

"Now there is nothing inherently startling in the things that I have been saying. The startling matter is that I should say them. The convention has grown up that, however important morality and faith may be, one does not mention them least of all in discussions of public affairs, especially economic affairs, and most especially in international economic discussions. This convention is western in origin, and like many western ideas, and especially western categorisations and compartmentalisations, I feel that it must be challenged. Morality and faith are relevant to economic progress, are part of modernisation. This is obvious once one thinks about it. So much the worse then, for conventions."

—Wilfred Cantwell Smith, Director,
Institute of World Religions, Harvard
University.

(From "Modernisation of A Traditional Society", p. 57)

When one knows Thee, then alien there is none,
then no door is shut.
The same stream of life that runs
through my veins
runs through the world and dances in
rhythmic measures.

—Ravindranath Tagore

We have tried to acquaint ourselves with the basic nature of Bhakti in the previous pages.

The culmination of devotion is Ātma-nivedana which signifies a sense of utter dedication and self-effacement. It implies losing one's personality in God. Philosophically it means effacing the ego completely and becoming the object of worship. Yes, it is possible to become the Supreme even through the pathway of devotion. Love-lorn Gopis became Kṛṣṇa in the highest flight of the emotion of affection. Ātma-nivedana signifies a metal stage where the self is wholly absorbed in the Supreme.

If realization of the Supreme is the ultimate objective of human beings, what is the harm if this aim is attained by and by through a gradual rise in ladder of spiritual progress until the topmost rung is reached. What is the harm if a person worships an image of his favourite deity, to start with, and then gradually rises to the highest spiritual position? Let a beginner begin from the concrete symbol. With the increase of his spiritual progress, he shall scale the heights and shall obtain the ultimate goal. What ultimately counts is the mental attitude. It is not very material if this attitude is provided by the fire of knowledge or the tenderness of affection and devotion. It is very clear to understand that the transformation of mind is more conveniently obtained through devotion, and accordingly the path of devotion is bound to be more popular. A devotee does not enter into any debate.[1] It is a crime to censure any scripture even.[2] The easiness of devotion is evident.[3] The toghness of the path of jñāna is well-known.[4]

It is therefore not difficult to understand this fact that devotion is more popular than knowledge or ritualism. It should not be presumed that devotion lacks the element of knowledge totally. We have already stated in a previous chapter that human mind is constituted by the three strands of knowing, feeling and willing. When we talk about devotion, therefore, what we mean is the predominance of feeling aspect of mind.

When there is a question of deciding the superiority, we shall have to concede that devotion is superior to the paths of knowledge and action because of its psychological feasibility and convenientness.[5] Ultimately it is the question of one's choice.[6] And since an ordinary man is likely to ask a question : "Where does the Nirguṇa Brahman reside ? Who is His father, mother etc. ? What is His complexion?" like the Gopīs of Sūradāsa[7] and is likely to insist like the Gopīs on being shown the Brahman[8], it is possible to know fairly well that the path of knowledge shall never be able to become very popular. It would always remain the privilege of a few. To quote the instance of the Gopīs, people in general shall proclaim that none understands the nature of the Nirguṇa Brahman here.[9] The result will be that for the vast bulk of humanity devotion is the only path of salvation. Love has its irresistible charm. An average person is likely to declare like Tulasīdāsa: "Let me steadfastly see, first of all, the King of Avadha. Only afterwards shall I listen to the talk of the Nirguṇa Brahman."[10] So intense is the attachment of a true devotee that he is not prepared to leave the object of his devotion even if people consider Him to be just a human being.[11]

As for the censure of the followers of the paths of knowledge, action or worldly life, the devotee does not care a fig for it. He would turn around and declare in a forthright manner: "Yes, we are the lovers of Gopāla; we value this love more than anything else; if you do not like this attitude of ours, we do not care at all for you."[12]

Thus no one can challenge the significance of devotion so far as the spiritual progress is concerned. But even apart from this spiritual significance, devotion has unique importance from the point of view of this temporal life. There are two aspects of our worldly life. The first aspect is the social life. And the second aspect is the individual aspect. Both these aspects are quite inter-connected and inter-related. Devotion enriches both these aspects of worldly life to a very desirable extent.

If we just cast a glance at the social history of mankind we shall easily realize the magnificent contribution made by the people who were devoted to God. A prosperous society can come into being only when the individuals constituting it are free from the traces of selfishness and narrow-mindedness and are the well-wishers of whole mankind.

Devotion has a tendency of transforming the human heart in a very revolutionary manner. The whole perspective of life is changed. His only objective is to be of sincere service to human beings, nay all beings.[13] Humanity is his God.[14] The inner desire of a devotee is to destroy the sense of pride and ego. For example Ravindranath Tagore prays in one of his famous compositions : "Lord, let me bow my head under the soil of your feet, let my pride be dissolved in the water of my eyes. I have tried to insult you by attaching importance to my own self. I have lived every second within the confines my own petty self. O Lord, please grant me this wish that I may not advertise myself in my actions and I may see your wish fulfilled in my own life. I long for your supreme peace, I crave to see your lusture in my life. Lord, please stand in the lotus of my heart behind me."[15]

From the point of view of social life, what is important is a heart that is full of good wishes for all and is dedicated to the well-being of one and all. Knowledge or salvation or ascetic life that is untouched with this type of dedication to the ideal of social growth, has no importance. Cānakya Nīty which is said to have been written by Cānakya, the famous founder of Maurya Dynasty after eradicating the Nanda dynasty completely, and a scholar and man of practical life, has drawn attention of all to this important aspect of social life. If an individual has a kind heart that extends sympathy to all beings, he does not need any knowledge, or salvation or ascetic life. He has already gone beyond them and has attained the ideal of social life.[16]

The devotees have a natural urge of helping others. The famous verse of Narasī Mehatā which was sung daily in the prayers of Mahātmā Gāndhi stated that only that man can be said to belong to God who feels the pain of others.[17] The works on Bhakti have enumerated 64 kinds of sins from which a true devotee must abstain. The most important sin is, of course, to tease any being or not to maintain any needy person or civilized individual.[18]

For a truly devout heart God is present merely in the form of human beings. "They do not recognise Him," maintains Ravindranath Tagore, "who is humanity in man."[19] Tagore also prays in his Gitānjali :

"This is my prayer to thee, my Lord,
give me the strength to make my love fruitful in service."[20]

and still further :

"Give me the strength never to disown the poor"[21]

In another poem he writes :

"Here is thy footstool and there rest thy feet
where live the poorest, and lowliest, and lost.
When I try to bow to thee,
my obeissance cannot reach down to the depth
where thy feet rest among the poorest, and lowliest, and lost.
Pride can never approach to where thou walkest
in the clothes of the humble
among the poorest, and lowliest, and lost.
My heart can never find its way
to where thou keepest company with the companionless
among the poorest, the lowliest, and the lost."[22]

A true devotee has no other desire but to serve humanity in a most disinterested manner. He lays down his life smilingly to please his God whom he sees in the lowly and the lost. Humanity is grateful to the host of people who were devotees of the Supreme and dedicated their whole life to help the poor and the needy. The names of Christ, Mohammad, Gandhi, Tolstoy and a host of others are too wellknown to be mentioned here.

Apart from enriching the social life, bhakti has a tendency of making individual life happy and contented. A true devotee has immense and unswerving faith in God. This is the secret of his strength. James H. Leuba, a famous author, has written about the psychological secret of this attitude." "Under the pressure of his need for help, man adds to them (i.e. the conceptions of gods) the desirable qualities and powers which he himself lacks, so that they may be able to gratify every one of his desires," writes Leuba, "Thus by objectifying his ideals in gods, originally due to an effort to explain striking experiences, and in entering into social relations with them, man actually accomplishes the miracle of lifting himself up by his boot-straps; he gets from his relation with gods something at least of the wealth with which he has endowed them."[23] A devotee believes that God would set everything right for him and no harm can be done to his self.[24] Therefore a devotee is never perturbed by any fear or threat or act of violence or anything else of the type. Jung, a celebrated writer of psychology and the founder of Analytical Psychology has written: "I therefore consider the religious teaching of a life hereafter consonant with the standpoint of psychic hygiene."[25] A person who has completely surrendered himself at the mercy of God, for him how there can be any worry or problem? He is happy in whatever condition he finds himself. A poet has written:" O Lord, may your will alone prevail. May my existence be completely merged in you. May there not be any other desire in my mind. As long as I live in this world, may I aspire for you and talk about you alone."[26]

There is one old Christian song stating:

"What a friend we have in Jesus,
All our sins and griefs to bear.
What a privilege to carry
Everything to God in prayer.
Oh, what peace we often forfeit,
Oh, what needless pain we bear,
All because we do not carry
Everything to God in prayer."

Faith healing provides an instance of the unconscious striving of a human being to go beyond the frontiers of his limited possibilities and capacities. In olden period the mental deviants were cured by the priests. History records that the mentally diseased used to visit the healing temples of ancient Greece and Egypt and they were cured by incantations and religious rites. At that time the abnormal were considered to be possessed by the devil which was driven out by exorcism, prayer, and sprinkling of subject with holy water. In this context it would be proper to quote C.G. Jung once again :

"Religion is a 'revealed' way of salvation. Its ideas are products of a preconscious knowledge which always and everywhere expresses itself in symbols. Even if our intellect does not grasp them, they still work, because our unconscious acknowledges them as exponents of universal psychic facts. For this reason faith is enough if it is there. Every extension and intensification of rational consciousness, however, leads us further away from the sources of the symbols, and by its ascendency prevents us from understanding them. . . .If we understand these things for what they are, as symbols, then we can only marvel at the unfathomable wisdom that it is in them and be grateful to the institution which has not only conserved them, but developed them dogmatically."[27]

The reason is obvious. For a true devotee nothing in life can constitute any disturbing factor, pain and pleasure, joy and sorrow, death and birth, everything he accepts with equanimity. His prayer is:

"Give me to drink each joy and pain
Which thine eternal hand can mete,
For my insatiate soul would drain
Earth's utmost bitter, utmost sweet."[28]

How correctly Milton has stated:

"Mind in its own place and in itself,
Can make heaven of hell and hell of heaven."

And since the faith in the Almighty transforms the mind completely, nothing upsets a man of devotion. Let us not forget even for a moment that thought is the material out of which things are made. In this connection a reference to the various miraculous experiences of the persons of faith may be made. The Klāyāṇa in its 'Bhagavannāma Mahimā Aura Prārthanā Aṅka" has reported many cases of cure from diseases, successes in the examinations, helps of various kinds.[29]

We thus find that devotion is of extreme help both in the spiritual growth and development[30] of the individual as well as his mental and psychological soundness. Thus both the society and the individual profit immensely due to an attitude of devotion and dedication.

The present condition of the world is fraught with a very serious conditicn and grave situation. The inventions of the Atom-bomb and the H-bomb have threatened the very existence of mankind. In the month of June of the year 1945 seven most prominent scientists of America had produced a famous report called The Franck Report which had stated: "The success which we have achieved in the development of nuclear power is fraught with infinitely greater dangers than were all the inventions of the past."

That this was not an idle speculation of certain inexperienced scientists was proved when in January, 1958 9,235 scientists of the world addressed a joint letter to the Secretary

General of the U.N. for stopping the atomic tests.[31] I have already written at length on this point in my published works Samaja Darshana in Hindi[32] and "Peace, Philosophy, And Progress."[33]

For example, I quote from my work "Peace, Philosophy, And Progress" :

"Is it not a sad comment upon the rationality of humanity that the money that should be spent for the betterment of mankind is wasted for thermo-nuclear annihilation ? When the bulk of mankind cannot find sufficient bread and clothing because of the shortage of money, money is spent like water to build sepulcher of the human race. And yet we call ourselves more progressive than our ancestors. What type of intelligence it is which is prompting us to cut that very branch on which we are sitting ? What kind of wisdom it is that is goading us to waste, in a moment of beastly madness, the treasures of human culture that have been accumulated through long centuries ? Today when we seem to be on the cross road of destruction and construction, we have to make our choice after deciding whether we desire to perish or flourish. And if we desire to flourish we must catch with strength that thread of unity of mankind which has slipped off our hands."[34]

At this hour when the individual life has lost its significance and human society is being thrown in the flames of destruction, what is needed is a devotee's heart which shall proclaim : "Who is my enemy ? With whom shall I now quarrel ? The Lord declares with His own lips : 'It is I who reside in every heart'."[35]

Yes, we need a devotee's heart who faithfully follows the teaching of God Śaṅkara :

"Umā dear, those who are devoted to the feet of Śrī Rāma and are free from vanity, lust and anger see the world as permeated with their Lord; with whom will they quarrel ?[36]

The Bhagavadgītā tells devotees :

"He who is free from malice towards all creatures, is a disinterested friend of all and is full of motiveless compassion . . . he is My beloved devotee."[37]

Our present position has been very well described by the following statement of Arjuna :

"Oh what a pity. Though possessed of intelligence we have set our mind on the commission of a great sin in that due to lust for throne and enjoyment we are intent on killing our own kinsmen."[38]

The misery and pangs of individual lives can be transformed into eternal blissfulness and ecstacy by cultivating the devotional attitude. Let us recall the words of Wordsworth on Tintern Abbey :

I have felt
A presence that disturbs me with the joy
Of elevated thoughts, a sense sublime
Of something far more deeply interfused,
Whose dwelling is the light of setting suns,
And the round ocean and the living air,
And the blue sky and in the mind of man,
A motion and a spirit which impels
All thinking things, all objects of all thought,
And rolls through all things.

A devotee that in the words of Coleridge realizes that God is

"Father of earth and heaven,
All conscious presence of the universe,
Nature's vast, ever-acting energy,
In will, in deed, impulse of All-in-All."

is quite close to him. In the words of Tennyson He is experienced as

"closer is he than breathing, and
nearer than hands and feet."

Devotion generates new confidence and energy in the mind of an individual. It needs no special talent, or beauty or any other special mark. "What righteous conduct did the hunter possess? Was Dhruva advanced in age? What erudition did the Lord of elephants possess? Did Kubjā have an attractive appearnce? What wealth did Sudāmā claim? Did Vidura claim any high descent? What prowess was exhibited by Ugrasena, the Yādava King? The Lord is pleased only by devotion, and not by merits; for He is fond of devotion."[39] The utter simplicity of the path of devotion has attracted even the lowliest to accept it and move steadily on the path of spiritual attainment of the highest type. His humble but sincere prayer reaches the Supreme more speedily than the exposition of any religious or philosophical work. When he addresses his prayer "O Lord of lords, I do not know how you are, what is your form? But O God of gods, whatever you are, I salute you, bow before you repeatedly."[40]

Nobody knows the ultimate nature of the Supreme.[41]

But the devotee knows His nature. Is He not his Beloved? And therefore every action of his is dedicated by him to his Beloved.[42] Devotion easily carries a man to the heights where knowledge cannot take an average man. A big bulk of humanity is bound to tread the path of devotion. The world abounds in Mīrā Bāis, Tualsīdāsas, Nāmadevas, St. Agustines, Rūmis etc. and not in Hegels and Kants.

"Men have addressed their eternal Thou with many names," writes Martin Buber. "In singing of Him who was thus named they always had the Thou in mind: the first myths were hymns of praise. Then the names took refuge in the language of It; men were more and more strongly moved to think of and to address their eternal Thou as an It. But all God's names are hallowed, for in them He is not merely spoken about, but also spoken to."[43]

We need a host of devotees who sincerely love their Lord, see Him in every being, and are prepared to serve the lowliest even at the cost of their social position, pelf, power and even life. The cause of humanity needs such martyrs who shall smilingly lay down their lives at the altar of humanity. Devotion is that light which brings about shine not only in the lives of discontented, tired and weary souls, but lights the blinding darkness and transforms social gloom into social gaiety and prosperity. A devotee does not care much for political dogmas. But he is best socialist, the brightest communist, the most shining well-wisher of humanity. Jacques Maritain has rightly observed: "If civilization is to survive, if the emergent civilization is to achieve the fulfilment of its potentialities, the coming age must be an age of spiritual as well as social integration."[44] Devotion alone has the potentiality of effecting this spiritual and social integration.

Erich Fromm has written about what he calls the "Humanistic Religion" in his work, Psychoanalysis and Religion.[45] What is important for us to note is that according to him "God is the image of man's higher self, a symbol of what man potentially is or ought to become."[46] And since devotee's God is kindness, generosity, helpfulness, etc. incarnate. He can be the best guide to humanity's march towards progress and prosperity.

In the West too this tradition of followers of faith is as old as humanity. The remarkable example of this faith is found in the life of Socrates who preferred to follow the voice of his God even on pain of being put to death.

"If you should say to me, 'O Socrates, at the moment we will not hearken to Anytus, but we release you on this condition, that you no longer abide in this inquiry or practise philosophy—and if you are caught still doing this, you will be put to death', if then you would release me on these conditions, I should say to you, 'You have my thanks and affection, men of Athens, but I will obey the God rather than you and, while I have breath and power, I will not desist from practising philosophy."[47]

The role played by faith is very great. One should not think faith is something opposed to reason, which is supposed to be the chief agency of human progress. Faith is not unreason or irrationality. It means transcending the frontiers of reason to realize and embrace what is beyond its domain, beyond the realm of rationality.[48] Faith is not blind. It has a vision of the Supreme. That is why a man of faith is man of rare humanitarian attributes and virtues. Omar Khaiyyam has pointed to the role played by faith when he wrote:

"Myself when young did eagerly frequent
Doctor and Saint and heard great argument
About it and about : but evermore
Came out by that same door where in I went.

....

"Then of the Thee in Me who works behind
The veil, I lifted up my hands to find
A lamp amid the Darkness; and I heard,
As from Without—'The Me Within Thee Blind' "

Faith is more reliable as it "is certainty of conviction based on one's experience of thought and feeling, not assent to propositions on credit of the proposer."[49]

God is born when this faith becomes alive.[50] And Devotion is embodiment of this faith.

We have by this time realized the glory of devotion. This very devotion has been the moving force of Indian life, literature, religion, philosophy, political ideal and culture. Right from the dawn of Indian civilization, devotion has played its prominent and constructive role. We have already seen how the elements of devotion are present in the hymns of Ṛgveda and the Upanishadic literature. There is no point in repeating it here. The very best literature of India was brought into being and was permeated with a sense of this very devotion. Bhāsa, Kālidāsa, Bhāravi, Bāṇa Bhatta, Bhavabhūti Sūradāsa, Tulasīdāsa, Kabira, Mīrābāi, Tukārāma, Narasī Bhagata, Caṇdidāsa, Vidyāpati, Ravindra Natha Tagore—the list is endless. Every literary figure was inspired by devotion.

One can find the role played by devotion even in the region of religion and philosophy. Religion in India was never a mere performance of rites and scriptural injunctions. It is the fundamental principle that sustains life—both social as well as individual. It connotes a mental attitude that revolutionizes the whole individual life. It denotes a transformation of life in the light of certain accepted principles.

"Religion is essentially a concern of the inner life." writes Radhakrishnan. "Its end is to secure spiritual certainty which lifts life above meaningless existence or dull despair."[51]

We should not be surprised to find the element of devotion present even in the religions like Buddhism and Jainism which do not believe in God. Aśvaghoṣa, for example, was a devotee in the domain of Buddhistic devotion. In his Bodhicaryāvatāra we find an example of an intense devotion.[52] We have already seen how Śaṁkara, the great follower of pure knowledge, expresses the feelings of devotion. In the field of political life also we find the same force of devotion exerting itself.

The kings of ancient India were devoted to God and served the subjects dutifully. Cānakya, Candragupta Maurya, Aśoka, Harṣavardhana, Kaniṣka all were persons of devotion. The classic work of ancient politics, the Mahābhārata, is full of devotional attitude. The entire Indian culture as a whole was inspired by devotion. Let us see the caves of Ajanta and Ellorā, temples of Khujarāho and Puri, Kanchivaram and Madurā and many such ones, and we shall have no doubt about the veracity of this assertion. The pages of Indian history bear eloquent testimony to this fact. In fact devotion has nowhere played such an important role in human life as it has done in India. Every important aspect of Indian life has drawn colour and form, beauty and life from devotion.

What is the outstanding mark of Indian culture. Our answer to this question is, a devotional attitude of life resulting in a humanistic ideal of society where the barriers of sects and colours, sex and nationalities are conspicuous by their absence. Indian history is a glowing example of a synthesis of many races and creeds. This capacity of India stems from the nondualistic ideal and to a still greater extent from a devotional attitude of life. It is difficult to imagine the fate of India in the absence of this synthetic spirit. Perhaps then instead of Indian culture there would have flourished many conflicting antagonistic cultures and India of today which acts as a beckon light to the world would not have produced Gandhis and Nehrus, would have given birth to Napoleans and Hitlers.

No one can deny that bhakti or devotion is an indigenous product of India. Weber's opinion that it has come from an outside nation to India is wrong.[53] Barth's opinion that "the movement of Bhakti was an indigenous phenomenon which had its roots in the religious thought of the Hindu" is correct.[54] He has put a very relevant query. "We have only to ask ourselves whether India had to wait until the coming of Christianity in order, on the one hand, to arrive at monotheistic conceptions, and, on the other, to apply these conceptions to popular gods such as Siva and Krishna. To deny this, and we do not hesitate to do so, is to admit that Bhakti can be explained as an indigenous fact which was capable of arising in India, as elsewhere in the religions of Osiris, Adon Cybele and Bacchus, at its hour and independently of all Christian influence."[55]

Senart too has given his firm opinion about Bhakti being an Indian product and not an imported concept. "Bhakti has certainly in India very deep roots," writes Senart, and proceeds to add, "It is much less a dogma than a sentiment, whose powerful vitality is attested all along the course of history and poetry. Already in the Vedic hymns the pious enthusiasm burst into vibrant expressions of quasi-monotheism; the passionate longing of the One penetrates the oldest metaphysics; the Hindus, and even Aryans, were largely prepared to bow down before divine unities. Many super-human personalities must have emerged from the religious fermentation which was working silently under the traditional surface and which assisted, along with blending of races, the increase of local traditions, and raised to the highest level figures such as Visnu, Krishna, Siva, whether entirely new or renewed by their unforeseen importance. For this there is no need of any foreign influence.[56]

It is not necessary to dwell at length on this point as we have already noted in the second chapter that the concept of Bhakti is as old as the Ṛgveda and the Upanishads of India.

What is essential for us to note is that this very idea of bhakti was given a powerful exposition in the Bhagvadgītā and the Bhāgavata. Influenced by this inspiring exposition, the three great ācāryas, Saṁkara, Rāmānuja and Vallabha not only respected bhakti, but went still further, and instilled its spirit in their works and lives. Saṁkara, though predominantly a man of knowledge, had a devout heart. He established four maṭhas like Jyotirmatha, Govardhana matha, Sṛṅgeri maṭha and Sāradā maṭha in the different directions. These places elicit bhakti and faith in the hearts of people.

Rāmānuja also gave a great stimulus to bhakti movement, "He systematized the emotional and theistic tendencies of Bhakti and determined the philosophy of Vaisnavism"[57] Rāmānanda, a disciple of Rāmānuja and the fourth of his successors, according to Nābhāji's Bhaktamāla.[58] He accepted twelve disciples like Ravidāsa, a shoe maker, Kabira a weaver, Dhannā, a Jāta, Sena, a barber, Pīpā, a Rājputa etc. They all preached the gospel of devotion in the common man's language. The walls of social distinctions and discriminations were pulled down by them. For example let us take an instance.

"Brother, from where have the two masters of the universe come ? Tell me, who has invented the names of Allah, Rāma, Keśava, Hari and Hajarata ? All ornaments of gold are made of a unique substance. It is to show to the world that two different signs are made, one is called Namāza, while the other is termed Pūjā. Mahādeva and Muhamad are one and the same. Brahma and Adam are one and the same. What is a Hindu ? What is a Turka. Both inhabit the same earth. One reads the Veda, and the other a Kutaba. Earthen vessels have different names, although they are made from the same earth. Kabir says : both are misled, none has found God."[59]

Tulasidāsa, the foremost poet of Hindi, too was influenced by the Vedāntic thoughts of Śamkara and Rāmānuja. But he was very much influenced by the Bhāgavata.

Similarly Vallabha influenced many persons. The most popular poets to be influenced were Suradāsa, Naṇdadasa, Caṇdidāsa, Vidyāpati etc.

The current of this devotion was not peculiar to the Northern India alone. In the Southern India, too, many devotees inspired by the Acāryas flourished. Nāmadeva, Jñānesvara, Rāmadāsa, Narasi Mehatā, and of course the Alwāras can be mentioned here to illustrate the point.

Thus bhakti as enunciated by the Bhāgavata and the many Acāryas and saints have played a very predominant role in India. Despite the differences of dresses, colours, languages and climates and creeds, India has a rare unity. This unity is the creation of devotion. Devotion has melted the distinctions into a throbbing unity of mind and has effected an integration of hearts because of which a mighty current of unity runs through the apparent diversity of India. It is not difficult to imagine the result if this unity would have been effected. Devotion has given a liberal heart and charitable temperament to the people. This has helped them in sinking their differences.

Devotion has thus played a most creative role in building the personality of India. Just as it has brought unity in India it would help the world in sinking the differences of races, cultures, languages, dresses, climates, colours and sexes.

Let us clearly understand the supreme significance of devotion in recreating the pattern of new humanity in nations and the world, and in helping people to realize the Supreme. Those who look down upon devotion simply fail to grasp its significance.

What objection the Supreme can have if an individual tries to move towards Him through the comfortable road scented with flowers and scattering charm everywhere as exemplified by devotion, rather than the thorny, mountainous, dull and drab path of knowledge ? Let us, therefore, pray for the supreme devotion of the Supreme for the golden future of the temporal and spiritual worlds. It is the supreme religion of man.[60]

Then the spiritually dwarfed man shall attain a rare spiritual height. The problems of individual abnormalities and international peace shall be solved automatically. Once it is realized that to serve humanity is the way of realizing God, as well as realizing the solace of heart and peace of mind, one shall consistently endeavour to tread the path of devotion and attain one's cherished objectives. A man of knowledge is likely to be indifferent to the world. He is likely to dismiss the world as an illusion, a dream. He is likely to retire to the jungle and meditate upon the Brahman for his soul's salvation. But a devotee prefers to live amongst the lowly, and serve them to the best of his ability. He shall prefer the service of his people, than the attainment of heaven or even salvation.[61]

Has Nānaka not said ?

"There are lowest men among the low, Nanaka shall go with them; what has he got to do with the great ? God's eye of mercy falls on those who take care of the lowly. Nonsense is caste and nonsense the titled fame. What power has caste ? Nobody is without some worth."[62]

Devotion is the glory of humanity. It is the best fruition of the spirit of dedication that brings the Supreme near and humanity closer.

This spirit of devotion has given Indian culture a very harmonious and melodious touch. Indian culture is certainly a synthesis of higher values. It is not centered on economic or some physical factor alone. In this context the following words of Aurobindo are worth quoting :

"The idea of culture begins to define itself for us a little more clearly, or at least it has put away from it in a clear contrast its natural opposites. The unmental, the purely physical life is very obviously its opposite, it is barbarism; the unintellectual vital, the crude economic or the domestic life which looks only to money-getting, the procreation of a family and its maintenance, are equally its opposites; they are another and even uglier barbarism We agree to regard the individual who is dominated by them and has no thought of higher things as an uncultured and undeveloped human being, a prolongation of the savage, essentially a barbarian even if he lives in a civilised nation and in a society which has arrived at the general idea and at some ordered practice of culture and refinement" (Aesthetic and Ethical Culture). Indian culture is as vast as the universe. It is sublime in thought. This is clear from the statement of the Bhagavadgītā "Whatever form a devotee seeks to worship with faith, I stablize the faith of that particular dovotee in that very from" (VII-21). Hindu culture is a world culture free from any trace of narrowness. The spiritual nature of Indian culture enables every Indian to think in terms of world brotherhood, which can be the only basis of human progress in the direction of freedom from oppression. Aurobindo has rightly declared "But brotherhood exists only in the soul and by the soul; it can exist by nothing else. For this brotherhood is not a matter either of physical kinship or of vital association or of intellectual agreement" (The Religion of Humanity.) This breadth of Indian culture has come from Bhakti or devotion because motions are stronger than ideas.

Thus Bhakti has not only brought melody to individual life, it has put honey in the heart of Indian culture.

References

1. Nārada Bhakti Sūtra 74.
vide 'tarkāpratiṣṭhānat–Brahma Sūtra 2-1-11.
'naiṣā tarkeṇa matirāpanīya' —Kaṭh Up, 1-2-9.
asa bicāri je tagya birāgī; rāmahi bhajahi taraka saba tyāgī
—Tulasīdāsa
2. vide the list of 64 crimes mentioned in the Vaiṣṇava works,—Prema Darśana by Hanumana Poddara, p. 144-146.
specially the crime number 22.
3. Nārada Bhakti Sūtra, 58 : anyasmāt saulabhyaṁ bhaktau.
4. Kaṭha Upanishad, 1-3-14 : kṣurasya dhārā niśitā duratyayā durgaṁ pathastat kavayo vadanti.
Tulasīdāsa:
gyāna paṅtha kṛpāna ki dhārā; parata khagesa hoi nahi bārā.

ramacandra ke bhajana binu, jo cāhā pada nirbāna
gyānavanta' api so nara pasu binu punch bisāna.
Bhā. 11-14-18:
bādhyamano 'pi madbhakto viṣayairajitendriyah
prāyaḥ pragalbhayā bhaktyā viṣayairnabhibhūpate.
Bhā. 9-4-68.
sādhavo hṛdayaṁ mahyaṁ sādhūnāṁ hṛdayaṁ tvaham.

5. Bhā. 10-30-3: priyasya pratirūḍhamūrtayaḥ.

na kucha thā to khudā thā
kucha na hota to khudā hotā;
ḍuboyā mujhako hone ne
na hotā mai to kyāhotā.

—Gāliba

bindu bho sindhu samāna
ko acaraja kāso kahai;
heranahāra herāna,
rahimana apuhi āpa mai.

—Rahīma

lāli mere lāla kī jita dekhu tita lāla
lāli dekhana mai gai, mai bhi ho gai lāla

—Kabīra

jita dekhau tita śyāmāmayī hai
śyāma kunjabana, jamunā śyāmā, śyāma gagana ghanaghatā chāi hai;

—Sūradāsa

6. sūradāsa jāko mana jāso, tāko soi suhāta.

7. niraguna kauna desako basi,
ko hai janaka, janani ko kahiyata, kauna nāri, ko dāsi;
kaiso barana, bhesa hai kaiso, kehi rasa me abhilāsī;

—Sūradāsa

8. tau hama mānai bāta tumhārī;
apanau brahma dikhavai udhou mukuta-pitāmbaradhārī.

—Sūradāsa

9. madhukara vaha jāni tuma sānci;
purana brahma tumhāre ṭhākura, āge māyā nācī;
yaha ihi gāon na samujhata kou kaiso nirguna hota.

—Sūradāsa

10. bhari locana biloki avadhesā
taba suni haun nirguna upadesā.

—Tulasī lāsa.

11. rāma, tuma mānava ho ? īśvara nahi ho kyā ?
viśva me rame hue nahi sabhi kanhi ho kyā?
taba mai nirīśvara hun, iśvara kṣamā kare;
tuma na ramo to mana tuma me ramā kare.

—Maithilisarana Gupta in his work 'Sāketa'

12. kavi ṭhākura priti kari hai gupāla so,
ṭeri kahau sune unce gale;
hame niki lagi so kari hamane
tumhe niki lage na lage to bhale.

—Thakura

13. parahita sarisa dharama nahi bhāi

—Tulasīdāsa

iśā vāsyamidaṁ sarvaṁ yatkiṁ ca jagatyāṁ jagat

—Bhā. 8-1-80

14. bhagavadbhāva sarva bhūti
heca jñāna dreci bhakti.

—Ekanātha

sīya rāma maya saba jaga jānī
karau pranāma jori juga pānī.

—Tulasīdāsa

15. amara matha nata kare dao he
tomara carana dhulara tale,
sakala ahamkara he amara
dubao cokhera jale;
nijere karite gaurava-dana,
nijere kevalai kari apamana,
apanare sudhu gheriya gheriya
gure mari pale pale;
amara yena na kari pracara
mara sakala kaje,
tomari iccha hauka purna
amara jivana majhe;

yaci he tomara carama santi
parane tomara parama kanti,
amare adala kariya dandao
hrdaya-padma-tale.

16. yasya cittaṁ dravībhūtaṁ krpayā sarvajantuṣu
tasya jñānena mokṣena kim jaṭābhasmalepaiḥ.
—Cānakyanīti

kabira āpa thagāiye, aura na thagiye koya
āpa thage sukha ūpaje, aura thage dukha hoya.
—Kabira

Bhā. 11-4-13.

17. vaiṣnava jana to tene kahiye
je pīra parāi jaṇe re.
—Narasiṁha Mehatā

sarvatrātmaśvarānvīkṣam (seeing God and oneself everywhere)
—Bhā. 11-3-25.

18. Hanumanaprasad Poddar, Prema Darśana, pp. 144-146.
19. Andhra University Lectures on Man, 1925, p. 48.
20. Gitanjali, 35.
21. ibid.
22. ibid, 10.
23. Editor Vergilius Ferm, Religion In Transition, George Allen & Unwin Ltd, London, 1937, p. 187.
24. teṣām nityābhiyuktānāṁ yogakṣemaṁ vahāmyahaṃ
—Bhagvadgītā IX-22

anātha kauna hai yahān
trilokinātha sātha hain
dayālu dīnabandhuke
bade viśāla hātha hain

25. Modern man in search of a soul, New York, Harcourt, 1933 p. 129.
26. mālika teri rajā rahe, au tu-hi-tu rahe
bāki na mai rahun, na meri āraju rahe;
jaba taka āi tana me jāna, rgo me lahū rahe
terā hi jikra ho, aura teri justajū rahe.
27. Psychology and Religion, p. 199.
Editor, Premanātha, The Art of Living, University Publishers, Delhi, 1963, p. 188.

28. Sarojini's Poem—The Soul's Prayer.
29. pp. 677-697.
30. Bhā. 11-14-25, 26.
31. *Vide* my book, *Samaja Darśana*, pp. 159-160.
32. published by Tulasi Sahitya S.adana, Indore.
33. published by M/s Sterling Publishers (P) Ltd., Delhi.
34. ibid, p. 12.
35. aba haun ka so baira karau;
kahata pukārata prabhu nija mukha so, ghata hau viharau.
—Sūradāsa
Bhagavadgītā XII-13.
36. uma je rāma carana rata
vigata kāma mada krodha;
nija prabhumaya dekhahi jagat,
kehi sana karahi virodha ?
—Tulasīdāsa
37. Bhagavadgītā XII-13.
38. Ibid I-45.
39. vyādhasyācaraṇaṁ dhruvasya ca vayo vidyā gajendrasya kā
kubjāyāḥ kimu nāma rūpamadhikaṁ kiṁ tatsudamno dhanaṁ;
vaṅśaḥ ko vidurasya yādavapaterūgrasya kim paurasam
bhaktyā tuśyati kevalam na ca gunairbhaktipriyo mādhava.
40. tava, tattvam na jānami kidrśo 'si maheṣvara
yadṛso' si mahesvara tādṛśāya namo namaḥ.
—Śivamahimna stotra
41. Bhagavadgītā II-29, māṁ tu veda na kaścana Bhā. 8-1-11
42. yat yat karma karomi tat tadkhilaṁ śambho
tavārādhanam—Sivamahimna Stotra
Bhā. 10-44-15.
43. Martin Buber, I and Thou, trans. Ronald Gregor Smith, published, 1937, T. & T. Clark, p. 75.
44. Jacques Maritain, A New Approach to God, Philosophy of Religion, editors George L. Abernethy and Thomas A. Langford, Macmillan, p. 224.
45. ibid, p. 58.

46. ibid, p. 65.

47. Plato's Apology, 29c.

48. Hari Mohan Bhattacharya, The Principles of Philosophy, University of Calcutta, 1948:

"The genuinely religious feeling is not collateral or coordinate with reason, but a superior conscious level which we may call faith or intuition and to which the mind of man rises on the flights of rational analysis." p. 329.

49. Erich Fromm, Philosophy of Religion, p. 60.

50. Tulasī's Rāma-carita-manasa, Bāla-kāṅda, v. 2:

bhavānīśaṁkarau vaṅde śraddhāviśvāsarūpiṇau;
yābhyāṁ vinā na paśyanti siddhāḥ svāntaḥsthamiśvaram:

51 Religion in Transition, p. 20.

52. Bharatsingh Upadhyaya, Baudha Darshana tatha anya bharatiya darshana, Prathama Bhaga, Bangala Hindi Mandala, p. 600-5.

53. Dr. Yusuf Hussain, Glimpses of Medieval Indian Culture, Asia Publishing House, Bombay, p. 4.

54. Ibid.

55. Oeuvres I, p. 193.

56. La Bhagavadgita, p. 35.

57. Glimpses of Medieval India, p. 9.

58. Ibid, p. 13.

Rāmānuja-Devācārya-Haryānaṅda-Rāghavānaṅda-Rāmānaṅda

59. Dui jagadisa kaha te aye kahu kaune bharamaya
Alla rama karima kesava hari hajarata nama dharaya;
Gahana eka kanaka te gahana ta me bhava na duja;
Kahana sunana ko dui kara rakhe yaka namaja yaka puja;
Vahi mahadeva, vahi muhammada brahma adama kahiye
Koi hindu koi turaka kahave eka jimi para rahiye;
Vedakitaba padhe ve kutaba ve maulana ve pande
Vigata vigata ke nama dharayo yaka mati ke bande.

60. Bhā. 1-2-6; 6-3-22; 4-31-9.

61. Bhā. 7-9-44.

62. Janama Sākhi; Bhā. 9-21-12.

Appendices

THE BHAKTI SŪTRAS OF ŚĀNDILYA

1. Now, then, enquiry into the Doctrine of Devotion.
2. The primary Devotion is the attachment to the Lord.
3. From the teaching (of the Vedas) regarding immortality of him who lives, moves, and has his being in Him.
4. Is it knowledge? No : because of the absence of devotion in the knowledge too of one who hates.
5. And because of the decay or disappearance of knowledge by her (Devotion).
6. Because of its being contradictory to hate, and because of the use of the word, Basa, (Devotion is) attachment.
7. No : Because, like knowledge, it also does not depend upon the form of action.
8. Wherefore its fruit is eternal.
9. It is not knowledge, because also of the testimony or verbal proof of attainment (in the case) of him who is possessed of knowledge, as is the case with attainment of others.

SECOND PART

10. She (devotion) is the principal, because the others are subservient to it.
11. And also from the topic under discussion.
12. Is it the result of "seeing ?" No; because of the intervention of the word sah (or he, in).
13. From observation also.
14. Therefore, in spite of the want of it (knowledge), (final emancipation) of the milkmaids (of Vrindāvana took place).
15. If it is said that (one) knows by devotion (as the Gita says); (we reply): Not so, because of the help received from the term 'Renewed knowledge.'

16. And previously stated

17. By this the alternative theory also is refuted.

18. The word "Devabhakti" refers to the Devotion to other (Gods) on account of its association (with the word Guru).

19. Again, the process of concentration of mind is for the benefit of both (knowledge and devotion), because of its necessity in both, as in prayāja (a sacrificial ceremony).

20. Attainment of Samādhi is, however, through secondary Devotion.

21. If it is said : (Devotion) ought to be avoided, because of its having the characteristic of attachment; (we say) No, for, like companionship, its goal is the Highest and the Best.

22. That alone, because of the teaching of 'superiority' to those that follow the path of Action, Knowledge and Yoga.

23. Because the superiority is established by means of questions and answers.

24. But (Devotion to God) is certainly not faith; because of its general use.

25. If that be the truth, (the argument would be fallacions) because of the absence of finality.

26. Brahma Kāṇda, moreover, refers to devotion, on account of their common attribute, its knowledge following (the other portion viz. Karma Kāṇda).

27. Application of the means (for the culture) of intellect (should be continued) till purity is complete to perfection like the continous striking (of paddy).

28. Of their accessories also.

29. Kashyapa thinks her (the understanding) (as) absorbed in the majesty and the lordship of the Deity, (to be the cause of final emancipation), on account of the supremacy (of the Lord over men).

30. According to Bādarāyaṇa, understanding when absorbed solely in the Atman, leads to emacipation.

31. However, according to Śāṇdilya, when the understanding is absrobed in both viz. the majesty of the Deity, and the fullness of the Ātman it causes the release, as is evident from the authority of the Vedas and valid reasoning.

32. If the objection is raised that the conclusion does not follow logically owing to the mutually contradictory nature of the two forms of knowledge, Śāṇdilya's reply is 'no', because there is no real contradiction, as is evident from an act of recognition.

33. The Supreme Reality does not become afflicted with pains and misery, because of the difference subsequent to the dawn of realization of the Identity.

34. To the objection that supernatural Divine powers (are) of the same nature, the reply is 'no', because those powers constitute His very nature.

35. The supernatural powers of the Lord are not denied (anywhere), because they are His very nature. This cannot be said in the case of others.

36. The objection that on the emancipation of everyone, there is no necessity of these powers of the Lord, does not stand, because the Buddhi or intelligence has endless limitation.

37. (The Lord) is immutable, as He works through the medium of Prakṛti (Nature), being ever accompanied with knowledge per se (His own self).

38. (The pharse) 'Firm basis on Him' (Firmly based in Him) is like (the phrase) "the seat in a room."

39. Because of mutual dependence, both Brahman and māyā or Prakṛti (are the cause of creation).

40. (There is) no third principle besides Brahman and Prakṛti.

41. And (both are ever) united, because both are without beginning.

42. The object of knowledge is not unreal, because it is (His) energy.

43. And the complete purification of her (viz. Devotion) is to be gathered from outward marks, like (that of the love of) ordinary men.
44. And (mark of Devotion to God can also be known) from the remembrance (of the acts of the well-known devotees from the fullness of their expression; (such as) honour, excess of honour (i.e. honour to those who resemble him in any way), delight, grief of separation aversion to everything else, singing His glory, preservation of life for his sake only, sense of belonging to Him only, the idea that He is the All, and Absence of enmity etc.
45. But hate etc. are not so.
46. Thus she (is) also (directed) to the incarnations, (as follows) from the last portion of the sentence.
47. Freedom from repeated births (is) of him who knows (the mysteries of) births and deeds of the Lord; (this follows) from Śruti.
48. And that is divine, as it comes into being only out of His own energy
49. His mercy indeed is the chief cause of (His manifestation).
50. (Devotion) to the manifestations of the powers of the Lord (in the created) is not (supreme or primary Devotion), because of (their) sentiency.
51. And from the prohibition of attachment to the game of dice and to kings.
52. Is it so in the case of Vāsudeva too? No, because of the (assumption of) the mere form (of Vāsudeva by the Lord).
53. And because of the recognition of Vāsudeva as Brahman)
54. That (is) because of His superiority amongst the Vṛṣṇis.
55. And thus in the well-known (incarnations).
56. By summing up worship with Bhakti or devotion (which is) secondary, because of its being the cause of Supreme or Primary Devotion.
57. And (secondary devotion is the effect) of others, because of the aid of the singing of the names of the Lord in the generation of attachment.

58. The latter in the middle; that which has the worshipped at its commencement, consisting of various parts.
59. From them, comes purity; from the (description) beginning with (the Gītā IX-2)
60. Some (say); By the additional use of the principal member, superiority in effect (is signified).
61. Jaimini (says), by name, because of consistency.
62. Here as regards the performance or practice of these accessories the proper time and appropriateness are as that of the materials in the construction of a house etc.
63. Even one of these accessories, (if) powerful, (is capable) of pleasing God.
64. Want of bondage, due to the dedication of all fruits of action to the Lord, is the entrance to devotion.
65. Concentration of mind (on the object of meditation) in the process of meditation (is) for the attainment (of its fruits) with ease.
66. The root Yaj (to sacrifice) is applied to (His) worship, not so to others.
67. Because of the fault of exclusion, (if otherwise), Pādo dakaṁ i.e. foot-water, signifies water for washing the feet.
68. Self-offered (objects) should be taken without distinction.
69. Rules of expiation (are laid down) for offences or sins due to carelessness (in the use) of means (of worship) as well as of the action (itself).
70. (Offerings) of leaves etc. refer to offerings (in general) otherwise, indeed, limited sense (would follow).
71. (These secondary devotional acts have) superiority over other deeds, from the fact that they are born of good deeds and from their being the cause of Primary Devotion.
72. The (first) three kinds are secondary; their mention along with the other for eulogy.
73. Lying both within and without, like Avesti, and sava.

74. Rules of remembering. singing of hymns, and narration of His attributes etc. (are laid down), as penances for the 'disressed.'

75. If it is objected (that there would be) the non-performance of severe austerities, even in the case of heinous offences, our reply is 'not so', because of its constant performance till death.

76. If the path of the devotee, an act of devotion, ever so slight, is destructive of great sins, because of its doing away with all the others.

77. Because it occupies its place, it serves the self-same purpose, like the post in a threshing floor.

78. Man, even up to the lowest born, has (equal) right (to follow the path of devotion), as it is taught by authorities one after another, like all other objects in common (with higher classes).

79. Therefore, indeed, by those whose devotion has not reached perfection (acts for its full development will have to be performed) in the Lord's abode also.

80. But the reaching of the goal is gradual or immediate, as has been demonstrated.

81. And 'gradual progress' (follows) from the concluding portion of Smṛti.

82. (The right) of the greatest sinners (extends) to the (devotion of the) distressed.

83. She (viz. primary devotion) is exclusive self-devotedness, as is clear from the recognition of the purport of the Gītā.

84. By performing primary devotion, the said (emancipation) is of all persons. This has been stated by the Lord.

85. This is not different from the object of devotion, as it has the same essential form as That.

86. His power is Māyā, because it has the common attribute "insentiency.

87. From the essential attributes of the universal principle, (those) of the particulars (come into existence).

88. Not from human intelligence, because it is impossible.
89. And having created the high and the low, He created the Vedas, like a father.
90. If it is said that this does not follow on account of mixed instrustions; our reply is 'no'; because they are very few
91. Result (follows) from Him, (states) Bādarāyaṇa, as is the result of observation.
92. Dissolution or merging (takes place) in the reverse order, as is seen.
93. That is unity; multiplicity or unity (appears) on account of the presence of upādhi or limitations like sun.
94. If it is said (that is) different; (we say) 'no'; because of the want of relationship of the manifested objects with the Lord.
95. Life is eternal; but there is loss of others from the absence of objects of enjoyment.
96. Rebirths and deaths originate from want of devotion, and not from want of knowledge, that being inconsistent with the cause.
97. Of these, there are three eyes according to the division of the Vedas, the symbol and the senses, like Rudra.
98. Appearances and disappearaces are modifications due to actions being joined with their effect.

NĀRADA'S BHAKTI SŪTRAS

1. Now, therefore, we shall expound the doctrine of devotion.
2. It is of the form of intense love for Him.
3. And it is of the nature of nectar.
4. By attaining which a man becomes successful, immortal and satisfied.
5. On obtaining which he does not desire anything, laments or hates nothing, revels not, nor becomes zealous.
6. By knowing which, he becomes overjoyed, quiet, and self-satisfied.
7. It is not led by desire, because it finds expression in (the) inhibition of all desires.
8. On the contrary 'inhibition of desires' means the consecretion of all customary and scriptural observances to the Lord.
9. (Inhibition) also means single-heartedness towards Him and indifference to all that is antagonistic to Him.
10. Single-heartedness (implies) the abandoning of all other supports.
11. By 'indifference to all that conflicts with Him' is understood the performance of those social and scriptural rites and ceremonies which are congenial to Him.
12. The observance of the sacred laws may be continued after the deepening of faith in God.
13. (The sacred laws should be observed even after faith in God has deepened), lest, otherwise, there may be a fall.
14. Social customs and usages also are to be observed only to the same extent (as scriptural ordinances). But, on the other hand, the occupation of eating, drinking, dressing, and so on, should be continued so long as we have to carry the physical organism.

15. The marks of devotion are now being stated according to different opinions.
16. Ardour or attachment in His worship etc. is the mark of devotion, according to the son or disciple of Pārāśara.
17. Garga is of the opinion that indulgence in talks of His glory and greatness is the sign of devotion.
18. Śāṇḍilya states that the indication of devotion is attachment in His worship and attainment of pleasure in the talks of His glory, provided that they do not hinder the enjoyment of bliss which the soul finds in God.
19. However, Nārada states that devotion is indicated by the condition of having dedicated all observances whatsoever to Him and by the feeling of extreme uneasiness on forgetting Him.
20. There are such and such instances.
21. As, for example, the cow-maids of Vrindābana (who, as stated in the Bhāgavata, dedicated all their actions to Lord Kṛṣṇa, and experienced extreme uneasiness when they did not find Him amogst them even for a moment.)
22. Even there, in the absolute fusion of personality with the divine there is no particular exception for forgetting the greatness of God.
23. Deprived of the sense of divine greatness, devotion is like the love of a woman for her paramour (which is constantly shifting from person to person, according as one appears more desirable than another).
24. In illicit love there certainly exists no corresponding feeling of happiness.
25. It is again higher than action, knowledge and concentration.
26. (Devotion is higher than other things) because it is its own reward, (whereas the followers of the other paths have ulterior objects in view, which necessarily separate them from God, and are, after all, finite in their nature, and therefore fail to secure abiding peace for the soul.)
27. (Devotion is greater than other means), because of God's aversion to egotists and love for modesty.

28. Some say knowledge is the source of devotion.

29. Others declare their mutual dependence.

30. The son of Brahmā states that devotion is its own fruit.

31. (What has been said above holds good), the same, and nothing else having been witnessed in the matter of feeling, bestowing favours etc. in the royal household.

32. For this, neither the king finds any pleasure, nor the recipients get any satisfaction of their desires (in the matter of distribution of royal favours).

33. Therefore, the path of devotion should be adopted, to the exclusion of the others, by those who desire emancipation.

34. The masters recite (as follows) the means (for the culture) of devotion.

35. But love of God is possible on the abandonment of all sensible objects and of every attachment to them.

36. (That arises also) from its cultivation without remiss, or from unflinching adoration of God.

37. (That springs also) from listening to and singing of the virtues and attributes of the Great God in society.

38. But that is obtained, principally and surely, by the grace of the great ones, or, in other words, from the touch of divine compassion.

39. Companionship of the great is, again, difficult to attain. It is hardly possible to assign how and when men may be taken into the companionship of the great. But once obtained, association with the great ones is infallible in its operation.

40. And companionship of the great is gained by the grace of the God alone.

41. Because there is no distinction between Him and his devotee.

42. Strive after love of God alone, try to get His love alone.

43. Bad company should be certainly shunned by all means.

44. Because it is the cause af lust, resentment, attachment, lapse of memory, loss of understanding, and utter destruction.

45. These evil tendencies, playing (even like ripples of water, ultimately behave as the stormy sea, when associated with bad association.

46. Who overcomes all limitation? Who conquers it? He who holds aloof from bad association, keeps company with men of noble hearts, and becomes selfless.

47. Who retires to a holy and lonely place, who roots out mundane bonds, who is beyond the three guṇas i.e. not swayed by them, and who forsakes both acquisition and preservation of worldly prosperity.

48. Who does not care for the fruits of his actions, who dedicates all actions to God and thereby becomes free from the influence of all contraries like pleasure and pain, good or bad, hot or cold etc.

49. He conquers all limitation, he overcomes all defects, and helps mankind to rise above their limitations.

50. The nature of love for God is incapable of being described in words.

51. It is like the taste of a dumb person.

52. It is revealed in some proper person.

53. Devoid of qualification, bereft of desire, growing in volume and intensity at every moment, and possessing a unbroken flow, it is a subtler experience of nature.

54. Having once obtained that, the devotee looks only at the object of his devotion, entertains talk only about Him, and thinks only about Him.

55. Devotion admits of three kinds as per one or other of the qualities of illumination, evolution or involution characterises the conduct of the devotee; or according to the class of the afflicted, the inquisitive, or seeker of knowledge to which a devotee may belong.

56. Each preceding kind of devotion works for the higher good than its corresponding succeeding one.

57. Devotion is more convenient and easy way of God-realization than any other way.

58. Because there is no need of any proof or demonstration in it, as is self-certifying.

59. Moreover, it fills the mind of the devotee with peace and bliss.

60. No anxiety need be entertained in respect of social dis-organization, in view of the fact that the devotee has consecrated his self and customary and scriptural morality etc. to the Lord.

61. Social customs and ceremonies need not be neglected in the development of devotion; on the contrary, one should surely attend to their due performance but surrender all consequences to God.

62. A devotee should not listen to talks about the conduct of woman, wealth and the unbelievers in God.

63. Self-assertion, pride etc. should be abandoned.

64. Having surrendered all his actions to the Lord, he should divert desire, resentment, self-assertion etc. towards Him alone.

65. He should keep himself away from the three modified forms of secondary devotion, and should develop love alone, which has its principle in those stages of devotion, which are known as constant service and permanent consortly conduct.

66. Real (primary) devotees are they who keep only one end in view.

67. Conversing together with a choking voice, with hairs standing on end, and with tears flowing, they purify their families as well as earth.

68. They make holy places sacred, they make actions meritorious; and they raise the scriptures to the status of good and desirable literature.

69. They become totally absorbed in the Lord.

70. Their forefathers rejoice, the gods dance out of happiness, and the earth becomes secure because of their devotion.

71. For them, there is no distinction of birth, learning, appearance, family, wealth, observance etc.

72. As they all belong to the Lord.

73. A devotee should not entangle himself in any discussion.

74. Because it can go on indefinitely and there will be still no certainty that it will ever arrive at the truth.

75. Treatises on devotion should be studied attentively and observances therein laid down as binding should be duly performed.

76. A devotee should not waste even half of a moment, because all the time one has for divine contemplation is little that remains after what is given to the thought and experience of pleasure, pain, desire, gain and the rest.

77. A devotee should carefully practise non-violence, truthfulness, cleanliness of body and mind, kindness, faith in God and revelation and other excellent traits of character.

78. The Lord alone should be worshipped invariably and whole-heartedly by the devotee who must repose absolute trust in Him.

79. He (the Lord) reveals Himself without the least delay, and fills His devolees' hearts with His presence, when invoked.

80. Devotion to the Eternal Lord is the most glorious thing; it is the greatest thing.

81. One devotion appears in eleven forms according as it takes the course of attachment to the attributes and greatness of God, attachment to His beauty, attachment to His worship, attachment to His memories, attachment to His service, attachment to His friendship, attachment to parental affection towards Him, attachment to Him (as) of a beloved wife, attachment to self-consecration,

attachment to self-absorption (or Godliness), and attachment to permanent self-effacement.

82. In this way the teachers of devotion, Sanatkumāra, Vyāsa, Śuka Śāṇdilya, Garga, Viṣṇu, Kauṇdilya, Śeṣa, Uddhava, Āruṇi, Bali, Hanumāna Vibhiṣaṇa, and others declare unanimously, uninfluenced by the fear of the observations of the crowd.

83. A person who entertains belief and faith in this wholesome doctrine expounded by Nārada, becomes possessor of devotion and reaches to the Dear of dears, the Dearest.

FROM THE BHĀGAVATA

1. Salutations to Him, whose glory sheds blessing to all; seeing, meditating, singing, hearing and woshipping Whom instantaneously removes a man's sins. (2-4-15)
2. I repeatedly offer my salutations to Him who kills the wicked demons and destroys the sins of the righteous: to Him Who is the repository of the pure quality of Satva: Who confers on those who have taken to the path of the Paramahaṁsa (liberated souls) the knowledge of the Self, which is otherwise attainable only by constant pursuit after it. (2-4-13)
3. May the adorable Lord, the protector of the good, the Lord of Lakśmī (the goddess of riches) the presiding deity of Sacrifices, the Progenitor of created beings, the Guide of the intellect, the Lord of the earth, of the world, Leader and Refuge of the Andhakas, Vṛṣṇis and Sātvatas (be pleased with me). (2-4-20)
4. I approach for help the son of Vyāsa, the preceptor of Munis who out of compassion towards the worldly men desirous of getting across the blinding darkness of ignorance, has revealed (this Bhāgavata Purāṇa) this light of the most ancient occult lore containing the essence of all the Vedas, possessing a unique greatness. (1-2-3)
5. That is a man's supreme Dharma which produces in his heart constant and unfailing devotion to the Lord (Adhokśaja—one who is beyond the ken of the senses). This devotion has no selfish ends. It makes the mind serene and happy. (1-2-6)
6. The Yoga of Devotion being devoted to the Lord Vāsudeva (Omnipresent Deity) produces non-attachment for mundane objects, and acquisition of knowledge wedded to the Lord. (1-2-7)

7. It is for this reason that seers practise constant devotion for the Lord, with exquisite delight which gives peace and security to the mind. (1-2-22)

8. Let the noble-minded person worship the Supreme Spirit with devotion, desiring nothing, praying for nothing, not seeking even the liberation. (2-3-10)

9. The Vedas have Vāsuveva as their sole object. The Vedic sacrifices are consecrated to Vāsudeva. The practices of Yoga and religious performances have Vāsudeva for their end. The study of the Vedānta and the Sāṁkhya deals with Vāsudeva. The performance of Dharma consists in propitiation of Vāsudeva, and the goal of man's life is the attainment of Vāsudeva. (1-2-28, 29)

10. The mind, distracted by mundane desires, does not get the condition of peace quickly through the restraint of senses and other practices of Yoga, as by the devotion to the Lord (Mukunda, one who confers final and lasting liberation.) (1-6-36)

11. His mind being purified and fixed by devotion, Vyāsa perceived the presence of the Lord, the Perfect Being, and also his power Māyā, in attendance on Him. (1-7-4)

12. The Bhāgavata Bhakti is superior even to Mokśa (emancipation). It quickly burns the subtle body (Linga Śarīra) just as the digestive fire in the stomach consumes the food that is eaten. (3-25-37)

13. But though My devotees may cherish no desire for subtle course of Mokśa being enraptured by the sight of My beautiful form, My surprisingly winning smiles, looks and sweet voice; their final emancipation is given to them as the reward of their devotion. (3-25-36)

14. These devotees of Mine entertain no desire for the enjoyment of the splendour and riches of Vaikuṇṭha (heaven) that My Māyā (power) creates for them, as well as for the eight kinds of superhuman powers (siddhis), yet all these gifts are conferred on them. (3-25-37)

15. Never will my devotees perish and be deprived of their joys in my peaceful abode of Vaikuṇṭha. For my weapon—the winkless disc of destruction—does not touch those who love Me as dearly as their own selves, their sons, companions and friends, teachers and tutelary deity. (3-15-38)

16. I carry them beyond the domain of Death—they who do not care for this life or the life hereafter, or wife, children, home and cattle or riches etc. They give up all other objects of value and are fervently devoted to Me. Death, the aweful terror, does not recoil from anyone except Me, as I am the Lord of matter and spirit, the Life of all beings. (3-25-31, 40, 41)

17. Therefore do thou serve the honoured feet of the Lord in every possible way with unfailing devotion such as is inspired by his excellences. (3-32-22)

18. That is Karma (action) which pleases the Lord, that is learning by which one understands Him and whereby faith in Him is generared. The Lord is the soul of all and is the cause, depending on no one else. (4-20 49, 50)

19. The gods dwell in him who has unselfish devotion to the Lord. How can the virtues of the great find room in him who cherishes no devotion for the Lord and hankers after pleasures beyond his reach. The ever-present Lord is the very life of all beings as water is to the fish. Though a man be great (in other respects), yet he can only claim his superiority as merely due to his seniority in years such as is the convention amongst householders if he is addicted to worldly pleasures and has forgotten his Lord. (5-18-12, 13)

20. Neither noble birth nor great fortune, neither eloquence, intelligence nor good appearance is the cause of Lord's favour. The Lord (Rama—the all pervading power) condencended to make us, the dwellers of the forest, his companions, void though we are of all the qualifications mentioned above. (5-19-7)

21. It is true that when petitioned the Lord bestows the object prayed for. But He does not give such gifts as would make the receiver desirous of making further petitions. He, of His own will, bestows on the devotees, though they have not asked it, the favour of His lotus feet which have the power of killing all worldly desires. (5-19-27)

22. This is the foremost Dharma according to the scriptures, viz. to offer devotion to the Lord by reciting His name and by other similar methods of devotion. (6-3-22)

23. He is a fool who takes shelter of any one else than the Lord, Who is not astonished (by His own greatness), Who is fully satisfied with what He has, Who is void of passions and therefore tranquil. The person who resorts to any one else for refuge wishes to cross the sea by taking hold of a dog's tail. (6-9-22)

24. The minds of men given to the wordly ways are not turned towards the Lord (Kṛṣṇa—the supreme power that attracts everybody), either urged by one's own inclination or by the counsel of others or as the result of exchange of thoughts of one another. Such men enter the dark regions of hell because they are unable to restrain the organs of sensual enjoyment feeding on them like cattle chewing the cud. They do not know that the Lord is the ultimate aim of life. Their hearts are fixed on thoughts and actions, setting a high value on the externals of worldly objects. They are like blind men being led by the blind bound by the chain of the ritualism of the Vedas. (7-5-30, 31)

24. The wise person should take to the Lord's devotion from early years of life. It is a rare good fortune to have human birth. Life is euphemeral and its short term should be made to yield as much as one can extract out of it. (7-6-1)

25. O scions of Asuras, much labour is not involved in the adoration of the Lord, who pervades like Ākāśa and is present in the heart of every being. He is the friend of

each and all. What is the good of procuring gratification of the senses, knowing as one does that such enjoyments are common to all living creatures (even to the swine that revels in filth). Wife, children, riches, cattle, houses, lands, elephants, hoarded treasure—all worldly prosperity is shortlived and can do little good to mortal man. These pleasures of the world (earthly and heavenly) are the rewards of religious sacrifices. They are subject to decay, they are not free from impurity; they create jealousy. Therefore, in order to reach the Supreme Being, worship Him whose blemish no one has seen or heard, with a devotion such as has been prescribed, (7-7-38, 39, 40)

126. Neither charity, nor ascetecism, nor sacrifices, purificatory rites, nor penance and religious vows please Him. He is pleased with pure devotion. Everything else is futile, mere mockery. (7-7-52)

127. I am of the opinion that neither wealth, beauty, learning, strength, energy, power and prestige, intellect and the transcendental powers acquired byYoga are qualifications to please the Lord. He was pleased by the prayerful devotion of the elephant, the leader of his herd (Gajendra) (7-9-9)

128. They who giving up devotion from which flows a stream of blessings, take pains for the acquisition of mere learning, get nothing but pains that they have undergone. They are like those persons who thresh mere husk and do not obtain food-grains as the fruit of their labour. O Thou, who fillest the immensity of space, many a Yogi, in olden times, having consecrated their practices to Thee, speedily reached Thee, their goal, by means of devotion which comes to them as the result of their Karma in the shape of listening to the narration of Thy glorious deeds. (10-14-4,5)

129. Here were the rustic women, who had their love firmly fixed on the Lord Who conferred His love on them. Indeed it is a matter of surprise that it should be so.

Verily the Lord readily lavishes His favour on His devotees, even if they are illiterate and uncultured. Powerful medicines effect cure of the patients from their diseases, whoever they may be. (10-47-59)

30. Oh, were I the wild creeper and herbs of Vrindāvana and obtain thereby the blessed contact with the dust of the feet of the milkmaids, who forsaking their family ties and leaving the regular path of social respectabilitv, clung to the feet of the Lord, sought after even by the Vedas. (10-47-70)

31. Thou art the Brahman, the soul of all, having an equal eye upon everybody. Thou experiencest thine own joys (not depending for thy joy on any external factor). Therefore Thou makest no distinction between people as being Thy own or as being other than Thine own. Thy favour goes to them who serve Thee; as is the gift of the celestial tree to him who approaches it with a desire, their rewards varying according to the measure of their service. There is no distinction in this treatment. (10-72-6)

32. Know ye the methods, which the Lord Himself, had laid down for easily reaching Him even by the unlettered and uncultured. Know them to be the Bhāgavata Dharma (the religion of devotion to the Lord) Following these methods, a man does nots werve from the right path. He can run with closed eyes, neither slipping nor falling. Whatever a man does with his body, words, mind or by the force of nature, let him consecrate it to the Lord by uttering the formula "To Nārāyaṇa" (11-2-34, 35, 36)

33. One should offer all desirable objects, all gifts of charity, penances, silent repetition of the divine mantras, good deeds and also that which is dear to oneself—wife, children, house, even life—to the Lord. (11-3-28)

34. Man has fear from his false perception of duality. One who is drawn away from God holds either the false idea of identity with the body or is forgetful of and does not care to enquire into his true nature; and this is due to the

illusive power of the Lord. Therefore man should serve the Lord with devotion, believing in the superiority of his preceptor; nay, in his preceptor's divinity. (11-2-37)

35. Who else than Vāsudeva can save men, who, blinded by the attractions of pleasures, have fallen in the deep well of mundane life and then devoured by that python Time. (11-8-42)

36. My votaries (states the Lord) though attracted by pleasure and unable to control their senses, do them by virtue of their strong devotion. (11-14-18)

37. Is is by constant devotion, O Uddhava, that one reaches Me, who am Brahman,the Great Lord of all the universe, the Creator and Destroyer. (11-18-45)

38. As the fire with its briskly kindled flames reduces fuel to ashes, so does OUddhava, devotion to me consume all sins. Neither Yoga (Karma-Yoga), nor Sāmkhya (Jñāna-Yoga), nor the study of religious scriptures, nor performance of penance, nor deeds of sacrifices win Me so much, as does the devotion, which is superior to everything. I can be known only through faithful devotion—I, who am the very soul of the saints. Devotion to Me sanctifies even the feeder on dog's flesh (the lowest man) and purifies him of the stain of birth and vocation. (11-14-19, 20, 21)

39. How can the soul be purified without the devotional emotions, without the pleasurable sensation of horripilation, the melting of the heart, the flow of tears of joy. Lost in my devotion, my votary has his heart melted and his speech choked (with emotion); he sometimes weeps and laughs excessively. Such a man of devotion sanctifies the world. (11-14-23, 24)

40. Just as gold, heated by fire, leaves off dross and regains its own appearance, so is the human soul cleared of its Karmic impurities by the application of devotion and attains to Me. (11-14-25)

41. Other patient toilers by means of the power of the control of their mind, subduing the mighty Prakṛti, become absorbed in Thee. They can attain the same result with little labour, if they choose the path of devotion. (3-5-46)

42. He who is the First Cause of the universe—its Creator, Preserver, and Destroyer, whose illusory power cannot be subjugated by great Yogis—He, the controller of three qualities, will adopt means for our well-being. What is the good of troubling ourselves with these cares ? (3-16-37)

43. I have no desire for Indra's heaven, nor for the position of Brahma nor for the sovereignty of all the worlds including the nether regions; nor for freedom from re-birth. Nor do I desire the power of Yoga, if O Lord, these involve abandonment of Thee. (6-11-25)

44. There are nine kinds of devotion : (1) the listening to the praise of the all-pervading Supreme Being (2) the chanting of His praise (3) remembering the Lord in meditation (4) serving the feet of the Lord (through His image) (5) worshipping Him through offerings of water, flowers, fruits etc. (6) salutation of the Lord (7) placing oneself at His disposal (8) making Him a friend i.e. reposing full trust in Him like a real friend (9) surrender of the self to the Lord. If one applies himself with this nine-fold devotion to the Lord, having learnt it from his teacher, I consider it as the best lesson he has received from his preceptor. (7-5-23, 24)

45. Hearing, praising, remembering, serving, worshipping, bowing, obedience, friendship, and surrender of the self—these are the nine forms of devotion to the Lord. (7-11-11)

46. The devotees of the Lord constantly hear, sing, pray, remember rejoice in His deeds of glory. They get the sight of the lotus feet of the Lord within no time, from which is produced the stopping of the flow of the stream of rebirths. (1-8-36)

47. Let our thoughts be fixed on the lotus feet of Kṛṣṇa; let our speech repeat His name, and let our body bow down in His salutation. (10-47-66)

48. The more is one's soul purified by hearing and singing the glories, the greater becomes the power of one's mind. One can then have the vision of the Truth, just as the physical eye acquires greater power by the application of collyrium. (11-14-26)

49. The Lord (the Endless) whose might is known to all, enters the heart of his devotees and drives away their miseries as He is praised in song by them. Just as the sun drives away darkness and strong wind drives away the clouds. (12-12-47)

50. The ears of those who do not listen to the glorious acts of the mighty Lord are mere holes (in the head). The wicked tongue that does not sing the hymns of the Lord, who is glorified by all, is like that of a croaking frog. The head, the highest limb of the human body, adorned it may be with a silk dress or a jewelled crown, is a mere burden, if it does not bow down before the Saviour. The hands, adorned though they be with gold bracelets, are lifeless like those of a corpse, that do not engage in the service of Lord's worship. The eyes that do not look at the symbols of Viṣṇu are like the spangles of the peacock's feathers. The legs that do not walk to the shrines of the Lord are like the trunk of a tree. That man is a mere breathing corpse who never places the dust of the lotus feet of Lord on his head, or who does not inhale the fragrance of the Tulasī leaf that had come in contact with the feet of Viṣṇu. (2-3-20, 21, 22, 23)

51. That is blessed tongue which is employed in the praising of good qualities of the Lord. Those are blessed hands which are employed in His services. That is the blessed mind which is employed in meditation on Him, who dwells in all movable and immovable objects. That is the blessed ear that is employed in hearing the glorious acts of the Lord which sanctify the soul. That is the

blessed head which bows down to his two-fold symbols—His images and His devotees. That is the blessed eye which eagerly looks at them. Those are the blessed limbs which purify themselves with sacred water with which the feet of Viṣṇu or His devotees have been washed. (10-80-3, 4)

52. The utterance of Thy name makes up all that is wanting in the invocation of a Mantra (whether due to wrong pronouncement or pronunciation) or wanting in Tantra (due to wrong sacrificial arrangement) or wanting in place, time and materials of worship—all these short-comings are made by the utterance of Thy name. (8-23-16)

53. The Kali Age is the storehouse of vices. But there is one virtue in it. By praising Kṛṣṇa a person is released from his bonds that enchain him and he attains union with Brahman. That which is obtained by meditation on Viṣṇu in the Satya Aga and by sacrifices in the Tretā Age, and by service in Dwāpara Age, the same is acquired by singing the praise of Hari in the Kali Age. (12-3-51, 52)

54. Just as fire causes the disappearance of the bad colour of the gold due to the admixture of alloy, so Viṣṇu by His presence in the heart of Yogis, removes wicked thoughts. (12-3-47)

55. Just as the watering of the root feeds the trunk and branches, so the worshing of Viṣṇu serves as the worship of all including self. (8-5-49)

56. Nothing is unattainable to those noble-hearted persons who have taken refuge in the feet of the Lord—the holy shrine that drives away all troubles (from its proximity) (3-23-41)

57. O Vidura, how can the troubles of the body and of the mind, the evils that befall a person from the skies, those that have their origin in the elements of matter—how can all these oppress the man who has taken reguge in the Lord. (3-22-37)

58. O Nṛsimha, parents cannot always afford protection to their children (being either helpless or neglectful). Medicines do not always cure the sick. The ship does not always succour a drawning man in the sea. Such means as are resorted to for the relief of the distressed are not invariably unfailing and do not benefit those who have not secured Thy care. (7-9-19)

59. He is no wise man who seeks protection of any one other than Thee. Thou art grateful, friendly, truthful and affectionate towards They devotees—Thou who fulfillest the desires of all who serve Thee, Thou who offerest Thy own self to them, Thou who art ever the same suffering no increase or decrease. (10-48-26)

SWAMI VIVEKANANDA'S PHILOSOPHY OF DEVOTION

Swami Vivekananda is an outstanding man of knowledge that the modern India has produced. He interpreted the Advaita of the great Samkara in a very scintillant way. Because of his extraordinary mental power, he was able to understand the nature of the Supreme Truth in reality. He was a Sanyasi and opted for the path of renunciation. But due to his penetrating intelligence and natural intuition, he could grasp the philosophic background of devotion.

Devotion consists in cherishing consistent and profound love for the Supreme Lord. Vivekananda understood human psychology perfectly. Hence he stated:

"The grandest idea in the religion of the Vedanta is that we may reach the same goal by different paths, and these paths I have generalised into four viz. those of work, love, psychology and knowledge. But you must, at the same time, remember that these divisions are not very marked and quite exclusive of each other. Each blends into the other. But according to the type which prevails, we name the divisions. It is not that you can find men who have no other faculty than that of work, nor that you can find men who are no more than devoted worshippers only, nor that there are men who have no more than mere knowledge. These divisions are made in accordance with the type or the tendency that may be seen to prevail in a man. We have found that in the end, all these four paths converge and become one. All raligions and all methods of work and worship lead us to one and the same goal."[1]

Hence, Vivekananda's attitude towards devotion is quite logical and rational. Let us try to understand it.

Vivekananda has rightly stated that every religion, except the Buddhist and the Jain, contains an idea of a personal God.

And even the Buddhists and the Jains worship the founders of their religions "in precisely the same way as others worship a personal God." This indicates that no religion, at least initially can do without some type of worship or devotion to a higher being.

However, this devotion is not expressed in a uniform manner. In fact there are different stages of devotion. At the lowest stage stands ritualism. But even at a higher stage some type of symbolism has to be accepted, as the abstract God cannot be understood without an aid of symbols. In the words of Vivekananda "Anything that appeals to the senses, anything that helps man to form a concrete image of the abstract, is taken hold of and worshipped."[2]

This tendency of trying to understand the Abstract through the concrete symbols is rather innate. Even those religions like Islam and Christianity which do not subscribe to idol-worshipping, are compelled to accept symbols of their own like the temple of Kaba or the image of Christ.

Vivekananda emphasizes that there is nothing wrong in this approach, provided, of course, through this symbolism one ultimately reaches the supreme. Vivekananda writes, "It is very good to be torn within the limits of certain forms that help the little plant of spirituality, but if a man dies within the bounds of these forms, it shows that he has not grown, that there has been no development of the soul."[3]

According to Vivekananda, every religion has three primary things which we have in the worship of God viz. forms or symbols, names and God-men. Worship of name is universal in religion, as some type of ritualism. Vivekananda explains, "Psychologically, in the mind stuff of man, there cannot come the idea of name without the idea of form, and there cannot come the idea of form without the idea of name.[4] "That is why names have been exalted and worshipped in every religion. God's vibration is present in everything. But He is only visible, recognisable, in man" and "thus, man has been worshipping God through men all the time, and must do so as long as he is a man."[5] But real thing is devotion, which is born out of the thirst or longing for God. This longing is the vital and fundamental thing. Religion really speaking implies realisation of the Supreme through individual, personal experience. Ceremonialism is left behind, as it is no longer useful in any way. On the other hand, it may become an hindrance. An intense attachment to God is the sign of real devotion. Nārada Bhakti Sūtra has rightly defined devotion as an intense love for God (sātvasmin paramapremarūpā-2). This love is so vibrant that nothing more lovable can be imagined (amritasvarūpā ch.-3). Its taste is so sublime that a person derives ultimate satisfaction in it. (yallabdhvā pumān siddho bhavati, amrito bhavati, tripto bhavati-4). A person spurns even heaven. (Bhāgavata 11-14-14). Then there is nothing left to desire, nothing is left to be gloomy about, nothing is left to be envious of, nothing is left to be attached to. (Nārada Bhakti Sūtra-5) This God-intoxication is the most important thing. In the words of Vivekananda, "And this madness, this thirst, this mania, is what is called the 'awakening' to religion, and when that has come, a man is beginning to be religious. But it takes a long time."[6]

Forms and ceremonies, rituals and pilgrimages etc., preceding this divine madness are just the preparation for the development of real love for the Lord. Those ceremonies and rituals, if adopted in the right manner, destroy the impurities and prepare a person for the super-human love. Spiritual love can appear only when the human heart is cleansed from material wickedness and weaknesses. But how shall we know that our love for the Lord is real and mature?

Swami Vivekananda provides certain tests to judge the justness of that love. First test is that it should be devoid of any bargaining attitude. If a person prays God for getting something in return, it is just bargaining. "I offer you a prayer, and you give me something in return; that is what it is mere shop-keeping. "A real devotee does not seek any material favour from his Lord. He says; "If God wants, I give Him my everything, but I do not want anything of Him. I love Him, because I want to love Him, and I ask no favour in return. Who cares, whether God is almighty or not? I do not want any power from Him, nor any manifestation of His power. Sufficient for me that He is the God of love. I ask no more questions."[7] The second test is that a devotee is free from every trace of fear. He is not afraid of even God. The logic is simple. If anybody is afraid of God, he cannot love Him. Swami Vivekananda puts a pertinent question; "Can you frighten one into love? Does the lamb love the lion? The mouse, the cat? The slave, the master?"[8] Hence, real devotion has no acquaintance with fear of any kind. The third test is that for a devotee love is the highest ideal. Love is its own reward. The Nārada Bhakti Sūtra (no. 30) tells us this very thing when it states that the fruit of devotion is devotion itself. The Nārada Bhakti Sūtra (no. 6) clearly asserts that a devotee finds the well of delight in his own self, where the ripples of devotion are continuously dancing. May be the reason is rather psychological. A devotee projects his own ideas of supreme joy when he experiences joy in the love of his Lord. Vallabhacharya for example, has composed his famous Madhurāshṭaka wherein he says that every part of the Lord is exceedingly lovely—His lips, His face, His eyes His laughter, His speech, His conduct, His movement. He concludes the panegyric by stating that everything of that Lord loveliness is extremely lovely—(madhutadhipaterakhilam madhuram). Of course, the Divine Body is made up of pure sattva element. But what is significant is the fact that a devotee finds supreme joy in his experience of devotion. It is a joy which cannot be associated with any physical object. This joy is, moreover, everlasting and not evanescent in character.

The fourth test is that a devotee's mind is free from every doubt about the existence and strength of his Lord. Arguments and doubts belong to a lower level. When a person ascends higher on the scales of spirituality, he is no longer assailed by any doubt as to whether God exists or not, or whether He is omnipotent or not. Swami Vivekananda rightly states: "The lover has passed beyond all these things, beyond rewards and punishments, beyond fears and doubts, beyond scientific, or any other demonstration."[9] A devotee is so sure about the existence of his Lord, which he feels intimately that he avoids argumentations and disputations as wastage of time and energy. (Nārada Bhakti Sūtra-74).

It is not a sign of his weakness of logical faculty. In fact a devotee too sometimes indulges into an argument to prove the existence of his Lord. For example, Swami Vivekananda has adduced a new argument for the existence of God. According to this argument "every desire in human beings has been created by something which already existed outside e.g. light made the eyes, and the sound made the ears. Similarly "This desire for perfection for reaching the goal, and getting beyond nature, how can it be there, until something has created it and drilled it into the soul of man, and makes it live there."?[10]

Mahatma Gandhi, the Father of Indian nation was a firm believer in God. He felt the presence of God all around him. We may acquaint ourselves with his thought about God. He writes :

"There is an indefinable mysterious power that pervades everything. I feel it, though I do not see it. It is this unseen power which makes itself felt and yet defies all proof, because it is so unlike all that I perceive through my senses. It transcends the senses. But it is possible to reason out the existence of God to a limited extent.

Even in ordinary affairs we know that people do not know who rules or why and how he rules; and yet they know that there is a power that certainly rules. In my tour last year in Mysore I met many poor villagers, and I found upon enquiry that they did not know who ruled Mysore; they simply said some god ruled it. If the knowledge of these poor people was so limited about their ruler, I who am infinitely lesser in respect to God than they to their ruler, need not be surprised if I do not realise the presence of God, the King of kings.

Nevertheless I do feel, as the poor villagers felt about Mysore, that there is orderliness in the universe; there is an unalterable Law governing everything and every being that exists or lives. It is not a blind law; for no blind law can govern the conduct of human beings; and thanks to the marvellous researches of Sir J. C. Bose, it can now be proved that even matter is life.

That Law, then, which governs all life is God. Law and the law-giver are one. I may not deny the Law or the Law-giver, because I know so little about it or Him. Just as my denial or ignorance of the existence of an earthly power will avail me nothing, even so my denial of God and His law will not liberate me from its operation; whereas humble and mute acceptance of Divine authority makes life's journey easier even as the acceptance of earthly rule makes life under it easier.

I do dimly perceive that whilst everything around me is ever changing, ever dying, there is underlying all that change a living power that is changeless, that holds all together, that creates, dissolves and recreates. That informing power or spirit is God; and since nothing else that I see merely through the sense can or will persist, He alone is.

And is this power benevolent or malevolent ? I see it as purely benevolent. For I can see that in the midst of death, life persists; in the midst of untruth, truth persists; in the midst of darkness, light persists. Hence I gather that God is Life, Truth, Light. He is Love. He is the Supreme God.

But He is no God who merely satisfies the intellect, if He ever does. God, to be God must rule the heart and transform it. He must express Himself in every small act of His votary. This can only be done through a definite realisation more real than the five senses can ever produce. Sense perceptions can be, and often are, false and deceptive, however real they may appear to us. Where there is realization outside the senses it is infallible. It is proved not by extraneous evidence, but in the transformed conduct and character of those who have felt the real presence of God within. Such testimony is to be found in the experiences of an unbroken line of prophets and sages in all countries and climes. To reject this evidence is to deny oneself. This realization is preceded by an immovable faith. He who would in his own person test the fact of God's presence can do so by a living faith; and since faith itself cannot be proved by extraneous evidence, the safest course is to believe in the moral government of the world, and therefore in the supremacy of the moral law, and the law of truth and love. Exercise of faith will be the safest where there is clear determination summarily to reject all that is contrary to Truth and Love.

I confess that I have no argument to convince through reason. Faith transcends reason. All I can advise is not to attempt the impossible. I cannot account for the existence of evil by any rational method. To want to so is to be co-equal with God. I am therefore humble enough to recognise evil as such; and I call God long-suffering and patient precisely because He permits evil in the world. I know that He has no evil in Himself; and yet if there is evil He is the author of it and yet untouched by it.

"I know, too, that I shall never know God if I do not wrestle with and against evil, at the cost of life itself. I am fortified in the belief of my own humble and limited experience. The purer I try to become, nearer to God I feel myself to be. How much more should I be near to Him when my faith is not a mere apology, as it is today, but has become as immovable as the Himalayas, and as white as the snows on their peak?"

This long quotation from Gandhi makes this point clear that for a godly person, the best proof of God's existence is his own experience. It also shows that a logical proof of God is irrelevant and unnecessary for a person who has realized God.

Thus we find that a person of faith does advance arguments to prove the existence of God to the people of the world. But he is aware of the fact that argumentation has no end. Moreover, it destroys the valuable time. (Nārada Bhakti Sūtra-75). It is therefore quite natural that a devotee who experiences indescribable love for his Lord has no liking for argumentation.

But according to Swami Vivekananda the ultimate fruition of devotion takes place in the form of the union of the devotee with his Lord. Devotion naturally starts with dualism—the Lord and the devotee both having separate existence. But ultimately a man of devotion rises to the highest rung of devotion and spirituality, where the lover and the Beloved become united, both are lost in one indivisible whole. In the words of the Nārada Bhakti Sūtra (no. 70) the devotee and the Lord become one like the river and the ocean. The ego which separates an individual from the Supreme is cast off and a perfect union emerges. In the words of Swami Vivekananda the devotee then says : "I am you, and worshipping you. I worship myself, and in worshipping myself, I worship you." The Gopikas of Vrija became kṛṣṇa, they became the very image of their Lord (prayasya pratirūḍha mūrtayaḥ). This is the culmination of devotion. This is the point where the paths of devotion and knowledge ultimately meet never to separate thereafter. Radhakrishna has rightly stated in his introduction to his work 'The Bhagavadgita' that devotion is "to believe in God, to love Him, to be devoted to Him, to enter into Him."[11]

Thus we find that Swami Vivekananda in the modern period has elucidated the real concept of Bhakti or devotion. In his inimitable style and language, he has unfolded the philosophy of devotion that gladdens our heart and pleases our mind. A finer interpreter of devotion than Swami Vivekananda cannot be discovered in the modern period.

References

1. Vol. I, Mayavati Memorial Edition, p. 106.
2. *Bhakti or Devotion* Swami, Vivekananda, Advaita Ashram, Mayavati Almora, p. 2.
3. Ibid, p. 4.
4. Ibid, p. 8.
5. Ibid, p. 9.
6. Ibid, p. 16.
7. Ibid, p. 20.
8. Ibid.
9. Ibid, p. 24.
10. Ibid, p. 14.
11. *The Bhagavata*, Blackie and Son (India) Ltd., p. 66.

INDEX